UNLOCK

the Secret to Lasting Intimacy

UNLOCK

the Secret to Lasting Intimacy

The Song of Solomon Decoded:
Joy, Betrayal, Forgiveness, and Reconciliation

An In-Depth Study and Retelling Based on
The AMEN (Ancient Middle Eastern Nuptial) Theory™

KIM MOORE

Published by:
Tin Roof Publishing
Land O'Lakes, Florida

Printed in the United States of America.

Kim Moore, 3551 Parkway Boulevard, Land O'Lakes, FL 34639 or Kim@KimMoore.net
Cover Design and photo/illustration by Scott Howard
Interior Book Design by PerfecType, Nashville, TN

Some of the anecdotal illustrations in this book are true, but the characters have been given fictional names to conceal their identity.

The Hebrew definitions throughout this book are taken from www.BlueLetterBible.org. This resource consists of *Strong's Hebrew Dictionary*, *Gesenius' Hebrew-Chaldee Lexicon*, and previous Bible usage and translations, and from www.BibleHub.com, including the *NAS Exhaustive Concordance of the Bible with Hebrew-Aramaic and Greek Dictionaries.*

Library of Congress Control Number:
Kim Moore,
UNLOCK the Secret to Lasting Intimacy:/Kim Moore
Paperback ISBN- 978-1-7356599-0-9
RELIGION – Christian Living – Love & Marriage,
RELIGION – Biblical Criticism & Interpretation – Old Testament

CONTENTS

ACT TWO: POST WEDDING

They will rebuild the ancient ruins;
they will restore the places long devastated;
they will renew the ruined cities,
the desolations of many generations.
(Isaiah 61:4 BSB)

In loving memory of my Mom, Shirley Perez—
I hope you're playing mah-jongg on a crystal beach in heaven,
enjoying a thick, juicy burger . . . I told you I'd finish it someday!

To my husband, Doug—
I knew on our very first date you were "the one my heart loved."

To my little mermaid and precious granddaughter, Summer—
You are the joy and sunshine of my life.

ACKNOWLEDGEMENTS

Writing a book of this sort was like digging through and excavating ancient ruins and artifacts. Trying to piece it all together, as accurately as possible, was another challenge. It was daunting and could not have been done without the help and encouragement of so many.

First, thank you Heavenly Father for guiding me every day and every step through the brutal wilderness. Thank you for not giving up on me. I am humbled and honored to share the Shulammite's incredible story.

To my amazing husband and best friend Doug—without your constant wisdom, sacrifice, and tireless support, this book would not have been possible. Thank you for sharing my dreams and for walking this long, agonizing journey with me. I couldn't have done it without you. I love you.

To Mom in Heaven—thank you for instilling an intense, never-give-up attitude in me. For so long I couldn't see that you were showing me how to take an average life of nickels, dimes, coupons, risk and sacrifice and forge them into a legacy. I always thought we'd get to celebrate this book together. I miss you more than I ever imagined. I hope I make you proud.

To Leslie Albaugh—thank you for listening to me cry, scream, and rant through the grief and anger. You were there for me (again) through one of the darkest times of my life. Thank you for your friendship.

To my beta readers: Sharron Cosby, Kat Heckenbach, Leslie Albaugh, Sheila Shynski, Debbie Barnes and especially Barbara Frone. Thank you for your precious time, support, encouragement, and honest feedback.

Thank you: To my writing coach Janis Whipple for helping me get it organized and on paper. To Darcie Clemon, my developmental editor, for your keen and insightful input on such a sensitive topic. You challenged me to take the book to a much higher level. To Renee Chavez, my copy editor, for reigning in and organizing all the scriptures and resources. And for the boost I needed to use *Abi.* To my proofreaders Amy Owen and Mary Rathman for checking and double-checking every jot and tittle. To Kristin Goble, my interior layout designer for an impeccable, classy and elegant interior design. To Scott Howard, my cover designer, for transforming the vision in my head into a beautiful and brilliant cover.

Thank you to Ken and Barbie and June and Ward Cleaver for decades of friendship and allowing me to share your stories as part of my story.

INTRODUCTION

In recent years Christian women in all corners of the globe have hungered to identify with the women of the Bible on a deep and personal level. Numerous books have been written about Esther, Ruth, Naomi, the Virgin Mary, the Proverbs 31 woman, Sarah, Hannah, the Shulammite . . .

Whoa. Whoa. Back up. The *Shulammite*? Who was she?

Let me introduce you to the Shulammite (shoo-lah-meeth'), the leading lady of the Song of Solomon and King Solomon's beloved bride. This slender, teenage, espresso-haired girl has been ignored, misunderstood, and misjudged for centuries. I have been studying this lady for decades, and I would go so far as to say that the Shulammite may very well be *the* most iconic woman of the Bible. If that was not so, then why has the enemy—Satan—schemed so relentlessly to silence *her* story above all the other women of the Bible? What's in her message that he doesn't want us to know?

For more than a thousand years, the Shulammite's legacy has been concealed beneath metaphors, misconceptions, and allegories. And I am thrilled to revive and share this unsung heroine's story. Once you see it, you'll be scratching your head and wondering, *It's so obvious. Why wasn't this discovered ages ago?*

First, let me take a moment to explain what this book is not. There are dozens of books and theories on the Song of Solomon, and I promise you this book is unlike any of them. The Song of Solomon is not the tale of a "love triangle," also known as the shepherd hypothesis. This theory alleges that the Shulammite was in love with a lowly shepherd boy, but the handsome and powerful King Solomon seduced her away from the shepherd, into marrying him instead.

The Song is not a spiritual allegory between God and Israel. Nor is it a spiritual allegory between Christ and the church. Or is it? It is and it isn't. You will see what I mean as the book unfolds. So then, what is it, *really*?

The Song of Solomon is just what it says it is: an intimate love story told in song, made up of one analogy, metaphor, and euphemism after another. It may seem a bit confusing and challenging at first, but if you stick with it, you will see the pieces fall in place, and the mystery of the Song miraculously unravel. As a double bonus, the more you learn about the age-old marriage customs within the Song, the more your understanding of the Old and New Testaments will be enlightened.

This book is based on my own research, the AMEN (Ancient Middle Eastern Nuptial) theory. The AMEN theory™ is founded on three basic pillars:

1. ***Ancient Middle-Eastern marriage customs throughout Israel, southwest Asia, Persia, Egypt, and northeast Africa***. These long-lost traditions are literally the keys that unlock the story line embedded within the Song of Solomon.
2. ***Old Testament Hebrew.*** To test my research and theory, I studied the entire Song of Solomon in Hebrew. Every. Single. Word. Why is that so important? As you know, in the English language a single word can have multiple meanings. It's the same with Hebrew. Once you understand the ancient wedding customs and what's taking place in each scene, it isn't that difficult to figure out which Hebrew meaning is the best fit for that scene.

I have tried not to burden you with too many Hebrew definitions. My hope is that once you see how simply and logically the Hebrew definitions fall into place, you'll find yourself actually looking forward to and anticipating the meaning of the next word.

3. ***The Bible.*** Scripture defines scripture. I took words and phrases used in the Song of Solomon and compared and evaluated them with their uses elsewhere in the Bible.

The Song of Solomon (hereinafter the Song) has been shrouded in mystery and has baffled Bible scholars for centuries. If you've ever read or studied it, chances are you understood little if anything about it. Sadly, I've discovered that most Christians are confused and intimidated by the Song, so they avoid it. Some find it offensive and attempt to ignore it or explain it away. Still others try to sanitize the sex right out of it.

But sex and marriage are two of the first things God created and defined in the initial chapters of the Bible.

> So God created man in His own image, in the image of God He created him; male and female He created them . . . God blessed them and said to them, "Be fruitful and multiply, and fill the earth . . ." And God looked upon all that He had made, and indeed, it was very good. (Genesis 1:27-28, 31 BSB)

> For this reason a man will leave his father and mother and be united to his wife, and they will become one flesh. And the man and his wife were both naked, and they were not ashamed. (Genesis 2:24–25 BSB)

God doesn't make mistakes. He designed our bodies and wired us with desire and sexual chemistry. It was He who declared everything He had made—including sex—"very good." A lot of people think,

Well, if it's so good, shouldn't we be able to discuss it? You would think so. But, for the most part, we blush, tiptoe around it, and treat it like it's shameful. Which is exactly what our nemesis hoped to accomplish when he set his sights on the Shulammite and the Song. He knew full well that if he could undermine something as personal and private as sex and marriage, he could affect the entire world from the inside out. This, friends, is why he has been hell-bent on suppressing the Song and creating chaos around it all these centuries.

The Titus 2 Woman

The Shulammite's message transcends age; it will resonate with women in all seasons of life: daughters, mothers, wives, sisters, and grandmothers. Her saga begins as an eager teen, moments before her betrothal banquet. Then it takes us through her fairy-tale wedding, a heart-wrenching marriage, and concludes with her own daughter's betrothal and wedding. Not only will her trials and hardships touch our hearts, but her message holds the missing pieces and authority to free us from religious stigmas of the past. The Shulammite is our first example of a Titus 2 woman, an older woman teaching the younger "Daughters of Jerusalem" how to be pure and self-controlled, and to love their husbands joyfully, skillfully and intimately.

Which leads me to my Titus 2 soapbox. For decades, *male* pastors, therapists, doctors and counselors have taken on the role of teaching men *and women* about sex. Please understand me: counseling, sex therapy, medicine, psychology, and pastoring are all honored and respected professions, and if you have issues with sexual addiction, abuse, or trauma, I beg you to seek expert counseling. My objective is not to oppose or dispute these professions. My goal is to ward off past strongholds from being handed down to future generations by providing practical biblical education *prior* to marriage. And the best way to do that is by putting

Titus 2:4 into practice—older women teaching the younger women in marriage, family, and *intimacy*—especially intimacy.

Isn't that what young women ultimately crave anyway? To be able to confide in and learn from older, wiser women who have not only lived through their gender-specific challenges, but overcome them? Let's face it: there's not a male, living or dead (including Bruce Jenner), who can relate to PMS, menstruation, pregnancy, morning sickness, childbirth, and breastfeeding. Not to mention menopause, hot flashes and night sweats. Period. Maybe, just maybe, this is why God intended a woman be the one to discover and unravel the mystery of the Song.

The Male Agenda

I might be the only woman who thinks this way, but I doubt it. Whenever I read or listen to men teach about sex, I filter everything they say through the *male agenda*. Case in point, a well-known, highly respected male Christian author who I admire and agree with on most issues wrote, "If you're not willing to commit yourself to having sex with this person two to three times a week for the rest of your life, don't get married."

When I read this, I could hear men all over the world stand and cheer, "Preach it, brother!" That may be this gentleman's weekly quota for his marriage . . . but that number doesn't work for every couple over the course of a lifetime. If he can cite the book, chapter and verse, he used to come to this conclusion, I would accept it. If he can't, then it's simply his opinion and should not be imposed on other marriages. I can't help but wonder how many husbands or wives were guilted into sex because of this man's opinion.

Man-made rules such as these are dangerous because they promote legalism, and legalism promotes guilt. When sex is "performed" out of duty and obligation, the joy of giving fades and resentment takes its place. Now, instead of a lack of time or an energy problem, we have a heart and attitude problem on our hands.

Why Me?

So, what makes me qualified to write this book? I don't have a PhD. I'm not a therapist. I'm not a minister's wife, nor do I hold a position on any church board. I'm an ordinary wife, mom, and grammi with more than my share of faults and weaknesses. Believe me: I've asked myself, *Why me?* dozens of times, and the answer always comes back the same. God's MO has always been to use flawed, unknown, ordinary people. And I pass those qualifications with flying colors.

To my credit, I have been married to Doug, my high school sweetheart, for forty-plus years (which is more to his credit than mine). Doug will be the first to tell you I have never been a nymphomaniac who couldn't keep her hands off him. And no, we don't experience fireworks every time we jump in the sack. To the contrary, as you will see, we (mostly me) have had more than our share of trials in the bedroom. My only bragging right is that I have a tenacious spirit that is utterly convinced God's Word holds the answers to everything, and I simply refuse to give up.

But back to the book. Over the years I have developed an intense bond with the Song of Solomon, and I feel as if the Shulammite and I have become *kindred spirits.* It's my hope that as you get to know her, you will come to love and admire her as I have. Allow her courageous story to open your mind, touch your heart, and liberate your marriage.

READER DISCRETION IS ADVISED: The first half of this book (chapters 1–9) focuses on purity and preparing for marriage and are appropriate for young teens. The second half (chapters 10–16) includes mature sexual content and is intended for engaged, married, or sexually mature adults.

CHAPTER ONE

Kim, What Is Wrong with You?

Six months after our honeymoon, Doug and I were sitting on the living room floor of our tiny rental house. He was unusually quiet and noticeably troubled. He turned, looked me straight in the eye, and tenderly asked, "Kim, what is wrong with you? Are you gay?"

The room swirled. "Noooo!" I blurted out as the tears went flying. I was crushed. But here's the thing; I wasn't crying for *me.* I was crying for *him.* I adored Doug. We'd dated two and a half long years. And while we were by no means angels, he had waited patiently all that time only to watch his premarital fantasies sink like a cement block to the bottom of the ocean.

We weren't having sex every day and everywhere as one might expect of typical honeymooners. No, we were having sex in the dark and under the covers. And Doug was trying to cope with a wife who couldn't bear to walk from the bed to the bathroom without first wrapping herself in the bedsheet. That's how it began. And six months later, there was no sign of improvement.

The household I grew up in was strict and rigid. Sex was a dirty, unspoken taboo. I remember getting my first sex-ed lesson at age ten. I walked home from school for lunch and went to the bathroom. To my horror, my underwear was covered in blood. (Thank God I wasn't at school when it happened.) Certain I was dying, I ran from the bathroom screaming. Mom gave me a clean pair of underwear and introduced me to thick, bulky Kotex pads. Then we sat at the kitchen table. As I ate my lunch she proceeded to explain. This is how I remember it:

Mom: "You're fine. You're not dying."

Me: *Wow. That's a relief.*

Mom: "This is normal. You just got your first period."

Me: *My first what?*

Mom: You will get a period every month . . . every twenty-eight days."

Me: *This is going to happen every month?!! Are you kidding me? This is a nightmare.*

Mom: "If ever you don't get a period, it means you're pregnant."

Relieved to know I wasn't dying, and in a state of shock over this dreadful "period every month" thing, I was too zoned out to care or ask how a girl got pregnant. So I kept my questions to myself and walked back to school in a daze.

A couple of years later, I developed a secret crush on a male classmate and came down with an acute case of teen idol infatuation over heartthrob, David Cassidy. So my dad decided it was time to give me my second sex-ed lesson. In a stern and foreboding voice, he growled, "Boys only want one thing. So, don't. If you ever get pregnant, don't come home. Ya hear me?" And just like that it was over.

There was that unexplained "pregnant" word again. My curiosity left me no choice but to seek answers from my equally ill-informed girlfriends. I also received an earful of inaccurate information eavesdropping on junior high school boys talking trash on the bus. It's no wonder I suffered from such a warped view of sex.

I grew up in the '70s watching wholesome sitcoms, like *Leave It to Beaver* and *The Dick Van Dyke Show.* These picture-perfect TV wives led me to the starry-eyed notion that the way to a happy husband was a sparkling, tidy house and a mouthwatering dinner waiting to greet him every night. I never gave sex a second thought. Why? Because I had this naive, pie-in-sky idea that if I waited until marriage to have sex, God was going to miraculously bless my husband and me with a hot and passionate love life. That was Big Lie #1.

The short walk down the aisle in my Mom's wedding dress did not flip some imaginary switch inside my head or body. Nor did the two-hour drive to our honeymoon destination. As a result, our wedding night left me feeling dirty, ashamed, and ruined. And I was plagued with these feelings every time we had sex.

Meanwhile, the only sex education I gained at church was: "Don't deprive."

The chasm between "don't do it" and "don't deprive" left me feeling guilty when we had sex and guilty when we didn't. I was in a lose-lose situation. I was suffocating in shame.

After coming to grips with Doug's question, I set out to get help and answers. The big question hounding me was, *If God created sex, then what did He have to say about it?* I didn't want someone's opinion. I wanted answers—book, chapter, and verse. If you think finding biblical sex education is tough in the twenty-first century, imagine what it was like in 1978!

I'd been volunteering with a mature, married woman in our church nursery for several months. At the end of worship service, as we were tidying up the nursery, I attempted to broach this delicate topic. Ha! You would have thought I'd broken out in leprous spots. She couldn't get away from me fast enough.

Next I thought, *I'll go to a counselor.* As I flipped through the Yellow Pages my heart sank. You see, back in the '70s, all the counselors were men. There was no way on God's green earth I was going to sit face-to-face in a brightly lit office with a strange, red-blooded man and articulate what I couldn't do alone in the dark with my husband. As far as I was concerned, that was indecent.

Determined to save my marriage, I found a thin paperback on the Song of Solomon, and it helped—for a little while. It at least convinced me that intercourse was blessed by our Creator. I reasoned, *If that's God's way of bringing babies into the world, then it must be okay.*

Unfortunately, the positive effects of the paperback wore off and a couple months later the shaming, troll-like voices crept back into my head. So did the guilt. I read the little paperback again—and again and again. I wore that little book out. It took grit and perseverance to erase and replace my deep-rooted, mindsets, but eventually the book's short message stuck.

I didn't realize it at the time, but that little book became the catalyst of my lifelong fascination with the Song of Solomon. Yet even though it helped me through a rough spot, it didn't answer many of my questions, such as, *What about certain sexual positions? And certain days of the week, like Sunday? How often should a couple have sex? Is this normal? Is that normal? Am I normal? Is he normal? What about oral sex? And masturbation? And lingerie? And sex toys?*

With these questions still unanswered, I searched many biblically based books on intimacy. Most were full of ageless wisdom and godly advice for young brides on topics such as submission, respect, good hygiene, and physical appearance. Yet each one had a vague and generic chapter on sex and the importance of not depriving our husbands. But they didn't answer my questions. The few answers I did find left me more confused: one book would declare an activity permissible; another would say it was immoral.

Still others claimed that God was silent on my questions, which led to yet another question: *If God doesn't say, 'Thou shalt not,' does that mean it's okay?* That also depended on who you asked. So out of fear of doing something wrong, I abandoned my search and restricted our bedroom activity to what I like to call *safe sex-in-a-box.* A very small box.

Fast forward sixteen years, to 1994. Doug and I were in our mid-thirties and we had two teenage sons. During that time, we were very close to two couples. The first couple I'll call Ken and Barbie because they were adorable. They exemplified what every couple longs to be—stylish dressers, with slim, toned bodies and good jobs. They were also highly respected leaders in our church.

For the better part of fifteen years, the four of us were practically inseparable. Every Friday night we watched *Miami Vice* together, and football on the weekends. We even took vacations together.

Then, out of nowhere, Ken left Barbie for another woman. It blindsided and devastated not only Doug and I, but their families, and our entire congregation as well. We grieved their divorce and our broken relationship for months.

The other pair I'll call June and Ward Cleaver because they were the classic *Leave It to Beaver* family. Our boys had been best buddies since kindergarten, and we had enjoyed being neighbors for ten years. They lived in a picturesque lakefront home, owned a successful business, and were admired throughout our small rural community. Doug and Ward often took the boys water-skiing and fishing. They even coached Little League baseball together.

Two or three months after Ken and Barbie's divorce, Ward left June for another woman. Lightning had struck on both sides of us, and we were singed. It was a one-two punch that left us traumatized. If this could happen to these model couples, I was certain it could happen to us. We were not immune.

Several months later, after the worst of Ken and Barbie's divorce had subsided, Barbie and I had a late-night, heart-to-heart conversation. I had a burning question I'd been holding back for months. "Barbie, as you look back now, did you see any warning signs?"

She nodded and replied, "Yes, but everything else in the marriage was so good, I didn't think it mattered." She paused and then dropped a bomb on me. "Ken and I were only having sex once or twice a year."

She couldn't possibly have said what I thought she said. *Once or twice a year! Are you kidding me?* This happy, attractive, affectionate Christian couple was only having sex once or twice every 365 days! No kids, beautiful bodies . . . Doug and I had speculated they were doing it like rabbits. I was dumbfounded!

Driving home from her house that night, I thought, *Well, that explains it! No wonder he left her. Doug and I are regular. We're safe.*

Instantly, all my fears and insecurities about our marriage melted away. Then, over the next couple of days I did something no one should ever do—I began comparing our marriage to Ken and Barbie's. The more I compared, the smugger I felt.

The following Saturday, Doug and I were sitting at the dining room table, mulling over the conversation I'd had with Barbie, when I flippantly tossed a question at him that forever changed my life: "Well, we have good sex, right?"

Crickets . . .

I thought, *I blurted that out so fast he must not have heard me.* So, I asked again.

Silence again . . .

The silence must have sucked all the oxygen out of the room because suddenly I couldn't breathe. This time, all I could squeak out was, "We do . . . don't we?"

Doug didn't say a word. He didn't need to. His eyes said it all. They said, *Kim, I cannot tell you what you want to hear.*

The silence, combined with the expression on his face, was shattering. If ever I wanted to shrivel up and disappear, it was then. All those years I had convinced myself that as long as he wasn't deprived, he was obligated as a good Christian husband to be grateful and content. That was Big Lie #2.

The ugly truth of the matter was, we *were* "regular" . . . as in, average. Agonizingly average. Lukewarm, going-through-the-motions average. There was no creativity and very little in the way of deep intimacy. Up to that point I believed average was safe—especially when it came to sex. But here's the thing: average is *never* safe. Average is always teetering on the edge of disaster and failure.

What does average look like? Author and speaker Andy Andrews put it this way: "If you're doing what everyone else is doing, you're . . . average."[1] And as far as I could see, our marriage didn't appear to be as secure as our friends'—and they were dropping like flies. According to the American Psychological Association, 40 to 50 percent of marriages end in divorce and the rate is even higher for second and third marriages.[2] That's about as average as you can get, wouldn't you say?

To be gut-wrenchingly transparent, part of me was content hiding behind ignorance and fear. Let's face it: it was easy. It didn't take any

---

1. Andy Andrews, "Podcast Episode 75: How to Change the World w/ Special Guest Julie Borlaug," Andy Andrews website, March 8, 2013, https://www.andyandrews.com/episode-75-how-to-change-the-world-w-special-guest-julie-borlaug/.
2. "Marriage & Divorce," American Psychological Association, accessed June 16, 2020, https://www.apa.org/topics/divorce/.

effort or imagination. But Doug's silence changed that. In the wake of our friends' divorces, living comfortably numb was no longer an option.

This forced me to tackle the questions I had deserted sixteen years earlier. Without the answers to those questions, I had neither the permission nor the means for creativity or passion. I reasoned, *If God created our bodies and marriage—and He promises to give us everything we need for life and godliness [see 2 Peter 1:3 KJV]—then the answers had to be somewhere in the Bible.*

To me, it was a no-brainer. I knew the answers to my questions were buried somewhere in the mystery of the Song of Solomon.

I set my sights on the Song again, but this time I wasn't going to quit until I found answers. Who knows? Maybe in the past sixteen years someone had made some new discoveries. I skimmed books online. I googled articles and blogs. I went to my local Christian bookstore, sat in the aisle, and flipped through every marriage book they had. But it didn't take long to realize people were still bouncing around the same old theories about the Song. None of the interpretations made much sense, nor could they explain the Song in chronological order. And for some reason that frustrated me. After all, all the other books of the Bible are in chronological order, and if God is a God of order, why would the Song be any different?

In spite of the fact the overall book of the Song was a mystery, there were segments that stood out and seemed rather obvious. For instance, we know the Song is a story about Solomon, his bride, and a wedding. It's also crammed with hot and steamy words and activities—such as kissing on the lips, French kissing, embracing—as well as sensuous body parts, such as bulging breasts, a curvy waist, and slender thighs and legs.

Hmmm, I thought. *Are not all of these things components of sex in marriage? There's no way you can convince me the Song is a spiritual analogy about Christ and His church.*

And what about Song 6:13b–7:8? In this passage the woman in the story is wearing next to nothing and doing some type of seductive dance for her husband. This convicted the socks off me, along with a few other articles of clothing. I can't count the times Doug begged I treat him to his own private exhibition, to which I'd roll my eyes and mumble, "In your dreams," or, "That ain't gonna happen." Now I was grappling with the question, *If the woman in the Bible did it for her husband, shouldn't I be following her example?*

Prayerfully, I mustered up the courage to begin imitating the woman in the Song. I wish I could tell you the light came on and I instantly transformed into a frolicking sex kitten. Seeing what needed to change was one thing; making that change was brutal. Don't forget, I was the poster child for modesty—the one who couldn't walk from the bed to the bathroom without covering my thin, smooth, cellulite-free body. (What a waste. How I wish I could have a do-over.)

The path to seductiveness was awkward, even terrifying, and I felt utterly inept. I can't tell you how many times I bought lingerie that sat in the bag with tags on it for weeks or months before I worked up the nerve to wear it. But inch by intimidating inch, week by week and month by month, I crawled out of my comfort zone and learned how to use what the good Lord gave me. Doug's compliments, gratitude, and persistent encouragement gave me the fuel I needed to keep pushing through.

I learned to laugh through the embarrassments and flubbed my way forward. After twenty years of marriage, we were finally experiencing our stolen newlywed years. We were affectionate, flirtatious, and playful. We may not have been "doing it" every day, but we were doing it everywhere.

It was obvious that Doug's Cheshire cat grin had absolutely nothing to do with a sparkling house or delicious dinners. *Au contraire,* I could have served him peanut butter and jelly on stale bread three days in a row and he couldn't have cared less. When the Bible says that love covers a multitude of wrongs, it's not kidding.

CHAPTER TWO

How Did the Song Get Buried and Distorted?

No matter how you scrutinize the seventh chapter of the Song, Solomon's wife was unmistakably hosting some type of romantic dinner and getaway for them to enjoy. So with that understanding, I again decided to follow her lead. I have an ardent passion for themed parties, so I began dreaming up playful, romantic, themed dinners; first for our anniversary, then for his birthday, and eventually just for fun. Little did I know these unique parties for two would become the inspiration for my first book, titled, *Now That's Romantic!*[1]

Huge pallets of my new book were delivered and stored in our garage, where my husband's treasured antique car once sat. Eager to inspire the weary marriages of the world, with high hopes and expectations I enthusiastically reached out to women's leadership at local churches. What I thought would be welcomed with open arms

---

1. Kim Moore, *Now That's Romantic!: Intimate Themed Dinners for Romantic Special Occasions* (Land O'Lakes, FL: Tin Roof, 2012).

was emphatically rejected. Worse yet, it was scorned as "edgy" and "semi-pornographic."

After a year and half of steady rejection, I'd had all I could take. I came unglued. I stomped through my house, shaking my fist at God and shouting, "I never wanted to write a book, but I knew that I knew that I knew You wanted me to! I've spent five years and an obscene amount of money on a book nobody is interested in. Did I hear You wrong? Don't Christians read the Song? If they do, they obviously don't understand it. Why would You give us the Song if we can't understand it? Did the ancient Israelites understand it? I believe with all my heart they understood every word."

Shortly after my outburst, I had what I call a divine hunch. I heard a whisper. *It's a wedding . . . it's a wedding . . .*

Irritated, I lipped back, "Of course it's a wedding. Everybody knows the Song is about a wedding. If it was that simple, historians would have figured it out ages ago."

I almost reasoned my way out of it, but I couldn't let it go. I sensed something must have been overlooked. I began snooping around the internet, googling "ancient weddings" and "ancient Jewish weddings."

Nothing.

Then I googled "ancient Hebrew weddings," and a few intriguing pieces surfaced. But when I searched "ancient Middle Eastern weddings," that's when things got crazy exciting. All of a sudden I noticed that the activities surrounding the *betrothal banquet* fit into the first chapter of the Song. The custom known as the *carry* fit into the second. The *wedding pro-cession* fit into the third. The *wedding and consummation* fit into the fourth. And they didn't kinda sorta fit—they fit in perfect chronologi-cal order!

This was a huge! These ancient customs were visibly emerging as the framework and storyline of the Song. For weeks I told no one, not even Doug. I just kept digging hoping to find more confirmation. *Nobody is going to believe me*, I told myself. *They'll think I'm certifiably nuts.*

Finally, one Saturday afternoon, while Doug was relaxing on the couch, I timidly blurted out, "Honey, you know how I've been studying the Song of Solomon for like . . . forever?"

He nodded.

"Well, I'm pretty sure I figured it out."

He did exactly what I feared. He rolled his eyes at me as if to say, *Sure you did.*

Intimidated, I hung my head and walked away.

Over the next few weeks, while Doug and I were eating dinner or riding in the car, I shared bits and pieces of my fascinating historical finds. One day I'd go on and on about the betrothal; a few days later I'd explain the carry. The following week I'd explain the custom behind consummation. But I never got to my conclusion.

A few Saturdays later I approached Doug again. This time I pointed to the couch and in my not-so-submissive voice commanded, "Sit down. You're going to listen to me."

He sat.

I opened my Bible to the Song and laid it on the coffee table in front of him. "Remember what I told you about the betrothal banquet?"

He nodded.

I read the first part of the Song out loud. Then I said, "Can you see how it fits?"

He nodded again.

"Remember what I told you about the carry?" I asked as I read the following section of the Song.

Another nod.

"Remember what I told you about consummation? Can you see it?" I probed eagerly.

Doug sat in stunned silence, nodding slowly. Finally, he uttered: "It does make sense . . . It makes perfect sense."

If you haven't figured it out by now, Doug is a skeptic. So, when he bought into my theory, I went into a happy dance. But my dance was cut short when he swiftly added, "But Kim, it's *too* obvious. You can't possibly be the first person to have figured this out."

"I thought the same thing," I fretfully replied, "but I've looked everywhere. If somebody has, I can't find it."

His remark took me down another rabbit hole. If the Israelites understood the Song at the time it was written, what happened since that time that caused the Song to become so misunderstood and distorted? That question led me into Bible history.

Doctors and therapists agree: religion doesn't help sexual dysfunction; it causes it. In his classic book *Intended for Pleasure*, Dr. Ed Wheat shares an example of one patient's angst: "To him, sex was altogether separate from his Christian life. The sexual relationship was an unholy activity in his opinion and yet he continued it with deep guilt feelings."[2]

Nobody wants to admit it, but the church is riddled with men and women who share this poor gentleman's pain and misery. Christian marriage websites are inundated with comments from both husbands and wives expressing this same anguish. Where did these twisted convictions come from? How did sex get such a bad rap? Let's look back at church history and see what went awry.

The Dark Ages

Disclaimer: The following historical facts are not intended to offend any person or religion. They are provided for the specific purpose of identifying and exposing past mistakes so we can learn from them and prevent them from doing further harm.

---

2. Ed Wheat and Gaye Wheat, *Intended for Pleasure: Sex Technique and Sexual Fulfillment in Christian Marriage* (Grand Rapids, MI: Revell, 2010), 17.

For the record I'd like you to understand that I have no allegiance to any specific religion. I was raised Catholic. As a teen I attended a Methodist youth group and frequented friends' Baptist, Pentecostal, and Presbyterian congregations. For most of my adult life I attended the Church of Christ. Now I am a member of a non-denominational church.

Today when we think of "scripture," we think of a *book* called the Bible. But in the first and second centuries, scripture was in the form of individual handwritten letters and scrolls scattered from one end of the Roman Empire to the other. Did you know that during the Dark Ages all scripture, including these letters and scrolls, were confiscated and impounded? Here's how it transpired.

Shortly after Jesus' resurrection, the Roman Empire flourished and became the most powerful political and military dynasty on the face of the earth. It comprised 20 percent of the world's population, including the entire Mediterranean coastline, most of Europe, the Middle East, Israel, and North Africa.

Around AD 180, the Roman Empire began to crumble and the Catholic Church—the empire's sanctioned religion—stepped into the void, establishing a tyrannical theocracy. Hence, the Roman Catholic Church was born.

In AD 382, Saint Jerome began translating eighty books of scripture into Latin: thirty-nine books of the Old Testament, fourteen of the Apocrypha, and twenty-seven of the New Testament.[3] This compilation became known as the *Latin Vulgate*. The Vulgate was sanctioned the "official scripture" of the church, and by AD 600, all other articles of scripture had been seized and/or destroyed.

According to an article on GreatSite.com titled "The Pre-Reformation History of the Bible from 1400 BC to 1400 AD":

3. "English Bible History: The Pre-Reformation History of the Bible from 1,400 BC to 1,400 AD," Greatsite.com, accessed June 16, 2020, https://greatsite.com/timeline-english-bible-history/pre-reformation.html.

By 500 AD the Bible had been translated into over 500 languages. Just one century later, by 600 AD, it had been restricted to only one language: the Latin Vulgate! The only organized and recognized church at that time in history was the Catholic Church of Rome, and they refused to allow the scripture to be available in any language other than Latin. Those in possession of non-Latin scriptures would be executed![4]

To complicate matters, priests were the only ones who had access to the Vulgate. And since priests were the only ones who could read and write Latin anyway, what did it matter? (For more information on the Dark and Middle Ages, see appendix 1.)

With the vast majority of scripture destroyed and the Vulgate under lock and key, religious leaders had total autonomy and full political power to promote whatever doctrines or agenda they deemed truthful, some out of sincere motives, others for control and corruption. Kind of like the censorship we are experiencing with Big Tech and social media today. So, what does all this have to do with the Song of Solomon?

Everything!

You see, for the next *thousand years,* the Roman Catholic Church believed and taught that sex was dirty and evil. And they ingrained their convictions deep into society. Those convictions continue to echo through the voices of men and women today, much like Dr. Wheat's patient, quoted earlier.

One of the most influential thought leaders of the second century was a theologian named Origen. He reasoned that if the lust of the flesh is carnal and God is spirit, then the Song of Solomon couldn't possibly have anything to do with sex (see 1 John 2:16; cf. John 4:24). To support his objective, he rewrote and interpreted the entire Song

---

4. "Pre-Reformation History of the Bible."

as a spiritual allegory between Christ and his church, which is where the "Christ and the Church" theory originated. Referring to the Song, Origen wrote:

> Any man who lives only after the flesh, . . . not knowing how to hear love's language in purity and with chaste ears, will twist the whole manner of his hearing of it away from the inner spiritual man and on to outward and carnal; and he will be turned away from the spirit to the flesh and will foster carnal desires in himself and it will seem to be the Divine Scriptures that are thus urging and egging him on to fleshly lust! . . . For this reason, therefore, I advise and counsel everyone . . . to refrain completely from reading this little book.[5]

Roman Catholic leadership jumped on Origen's pious bandwagon and ingrained their contorted views into young women's minds during mandatory catechism class. Many historians assert that Origen was so fixated on the evils of sex that he ultimately castrated himself.[6]

Augustine of Hippo, a fourth-century bishop who helped shape the doctrine of "original sin," capitalized on Origen's theory. He lectured to the masses that Adam and Eve's grave iniquity in the Garden of Eden was none other than sexual intercourse.[7]

To further emphasize the Church's relentless sex-shaming, let's look at the English word *pudenda*. This word refers to a person's external genital organs, particularly the female vulva. This word originated

---

5. Origen, *Ancient Christian Writers, The Song of Songs, Commentary and Homilies* (New York: 1956), 22–23.

6. Cindy Irwin, "Marriage and Sexual Wholeness: Helping Couples Define Their Sexual Theology," *Enrichment* (Summer 2011), https://enrichmentjournal.ag.org/Issues/2011/Summer-2011/Marriage-and-Sexual-Wholeness.

7. Irwin, "Marriage and Sexual Wholeness."

from the Latin word *pudet*, which means "it is shameful?"[8] Coincidence? I don't think so.

To keep parishioners from falling into fleshly lust, the Church established stringent rules and regulations on sex. For instance, intercourse was to be reserved for procreation only and restricted to the missionary position. Sex was forbidden on "holy" days, and if you allowed yourself to feel the slightest inkling of pleasure, you were sinning. And sin required confession and monetary penance. In short, the Church began profiting from sex. Big time. Some even allege the Church put sex police in place. (And no, I have no idea how they "policed" it.)

This was an especially terrifying time for women because any woman who inadvertently expressed pleasure during lovemaking could be put on trial, judged a witch, tortured, and executed. Seriously! With laws like that, who needs divorce lawyers?

This oppression lasted a long nine hundred years. However, in the 1450s, a man by the name of Johannes Gutenberg invented the movable-type printing press, which would revolutionize the world. It was this very invention that produced the first Bible ever printed, a Latin Bible known as the Gutenberg Bible. In the fall of 1517, Martin Luther, a former German monk, read the Bible for himself and found that the teachings of the Catholic Church were not in line with scripture. He opposed the Church by nailing his *Ninety-five Theses of Contention* to the door of All Saints' Church in Wittenberg, Germany.

In 1525, William Tyndale, the spiritual leader of a reformation group known as the Lollards, was the first to print the New Testament in English. Tyndale was imprisoned for five hundred days and ultimately strangled and burned at the stake in October 1536. Tyndale's friend John Rogers, under the names Thomas Matthew and Myles

---

8. Encyclopedia.com, s.v. "pudendum," accessed June 16, 2020, https://www.encyclopedia.com/medicine/anatomy-and-physiology/anatomy-and-physiology/pudendum.

Coverdale, completed Tyndale's project and printed the first complete English Bible, known as the Coverdale Bible, on October 4, 1535.[9]

After being held captive for ***more than a thousand years,*** God's Word was finally back where it belonged—in the hands of common man. However, three major dynamics evolved during this thousand-year oppression:

1. Society was heavily indoctrinated into believing grossly false creeds, such as the "evils of sex" and "holy poverty."
2. Many of the ancient Middle Eastern wedding customs, which shape the storyline of the Song, had either morphed into unrecognizable forms or vanished all together.
3. The analogies, metaphors, and euphemisms God used to veil the intimacy of the Song became entombed in time.

We might be tempted to think that once the Word was made available to the public, these ingrained mindsets magically disappeared. Not so. Entrenched mindsets are as relentless as iron shackles. As a result, the Song remained cloaked in confusion and obscurity.

Some three centuries later, this die-hard mindset was thriving well into the late 1800s. This may sound bizarre and even comical to us, but the mere glimpse of a woman's ankle was considered so vulgar to Victorian prudes they covered piano and table legs with floor-length tablecloths to prevent men from lusting after them. I'm not making this stuff up.

In Ruth Smythers's 1894 book titled *Marriage and Love,* she wrote, "Give little, give seldom, and above all, give grudgingly. Otherwise what could have been a proper marriage could become an orgy of

---

9. "English Bible History," Greatsite.com, accessed June 16, 2020, https://greatsite.com/timeline-english-bible-history/index.html.

sexual lust," and "Sex when it cannot be prevented, should be practiced only in total darkness."[10]

John Harvey Kellogg, doctor, nutritionist and co-creator of corn flakes, quotes unknown writers in his 1879 book titled, *Plain Facts for Old and Young:*

> "The very lively solicitations that spring from the genital sense, have no other end than to insure the perpetuity of the race . . ."
>
> "It is a common belief that a man and a woman, because they are legally united in marriage, are privileged to the unbridled exercises of amativeness. This is wrong . . . Excessive indulgence between the married produces a great and lasting evil effects as in the single man or woman, and is nothing more or less than legalized prostitution."[11]

Moving into the twentieth century, only six short decades ago, during the 1950s and '60s, Hollywood considered it indecent for married couples to be seen getting into the same bed. (Hard to believe, isn't it?) Popular sitcoms such as *I Love Lucy* and *The Dick Van Dyke Show* aired Ricky and Lucy Ricardo and Rob and Laura Petrie bidding each other "good night" from separate twin beds. If you grew up on these types of shows as I did, it's no wonder we struggle with mixed messages about sex.

Because most of us feel insecure talking about what happens in the secret place of marriage, it's impossible to measure the far-reaching effects of this problem. But I am confronted with it every time I speak.

---

10. Ruth Smythers, *Marriage & Love: Instructions for Females on Courtship and Matrimony, with Tips to Discourage Sexual Advances from Husbands* (Guilford, CT: Lyons Press, 1894), 41, 44.
11. Kellogg, John Harvey, *Plain Facts for Old and Young: Embracing the Natural History and Hygiene of Organic Life* (Burlington, IA: Segner and Condit, 1881) 223, 225.

Each time I step off the platform, I'm bombarded with women who want to confide their sex-is-dirty stories with me. The more I speak, the more I'm convinced this is the norm, not the exception. Thankfully, the Song holds the truth and remedy to this problem.

Spread the Cure

The vast majority of sex education from the pulpit today continues to focus on the *don'ts* and the evils of sex: immorality, pornography, homosexuality, and so on. All the things you *can't* do, rather than what you *can* do. In an article titled "Human Sexuality in the Image of God," George O. Wood, former general superintendent of the Assemblies of God, stated, "By not talking about sexuality, we let the world—rather than God's Word—set the agenda for how we understand and practice our sexuality. By not valuing it—or, rather, by preaching only against sex outside of marriage and not for sex within marriage—we let the world caricature us as killjoys and pleasure haters."[12] After all, shouldn't sensible education of any kind teach both? In recent years a few pastors have attempted to teach that sex in marriage is a good, beautiful, God-given gift, but without a proper understanding of the Song, they simply don't have the scriptural clout to back up their claims.

Simple reasoning tells us if A is C, and B is A, then B must be C. In other words, if sex is a beautiful God-given gift, and if it's good to talk about beautiful God-given topics, then shouldn't we be talking about sex? When our words don't match our actions, our subconscious minds logically conclude that sex really isn't good—it's bad. This lopsided rationale sends out a loud and incongruent message.

---

12. George O. Wood, "Human Sexuality in the Image of God," *Enrichment* (Summer 2011): 32, https://enrichmentjournal.ag.org/Issues/2011/Summer-2011/Human-Sexuality-in-the-Image-of-God.

The Universal Law of Balance

You can't argue with gravity. What goes up eventually comes down. It's a universal truth. Another universal truth is the law of sowing and reaping. Some refer to it as *karma*. Still another universal truth is the law of balance.

Too often we conclude that if something is good, then more must be better. That's only true to a point. Somewhere along the line the scales tip, and even a good thing if taken *too* far becomes destructive. Bottom line, *anything* taken to an extreme disrupts the law of balance. Solomon put it this way: "It is good to grasp the one and not let go of the other. The man who fears God will avoid all extremes" (Ecclesiastes 7:18).

As early as elementary school, we are taught to drink at least eight glasses of water a day to purify, hydrate, and cool our bodies. But can something as wholesome as water ever be bad for us? A true-but-tragic story shows that it indeed can.

In 2007 a young California mother entered a water-drinking contest at a local radio station in an attempt to win a Wii console for her children. Whoever could drink and hold the most water would win the Wii. This young mom chugged multiple pints of water in a short period of time.

On her way home from the station, she called her mother, complaining of severe head pain. She made it home, but died shortly after.

An autopsy revealed that this healthy woman had died from water intoxication.[13] Water poisoning occurs when the normal balance of electrolytes in the body are pushed outside safe limits by *extreme* hydration, creating a fatal disturbance of brain function. Similar tragedies

---

13. Associated Press, "Woman Dies after Being in Water-Drinking Contest," *Los Angeles Times*, January 14, 2007, https://www.latimes.com/archives/la-xpm-2007-jan-14-me-water14-story.html.

have taken the lives of a twenty-two-year-old college student in a fraternity hazing event, and a seventeen-year-old Georgia high school football player.[14] Crazy, isn't it? These unsuspecting individuals poisoned their bodies with the very thing created to purify it.

I can't think of a single example where the law of balance doesn't apply. Not one. Flood versus drought, obesity versus anorexia, workaholic versus sloth, miser versus credit card junkie, legalism versus hyper-grace . . . all extremes are dangerous, and sex is not exempt. The secular world has taken an *extreme* liberal approach, boasting about it anywhere and everywhere, while religion has taken an *extreme* conservative approach, avoiding it at all costs. Both extremes are dangerous and foolish.

In the previously cited *Enrichment* journal article "Marriage and Sexual Wholeness," Christian sex therapist Cindy Irwin shares Wendy and Eric's real-life story:

> Wendy was struggling with never wanting to have sex. She said she had been a good "True Love Waits" teen. Their first kiss was at their wedding. They have been married 4 years and never consummated their marriage. Truth be told, she hated even the idea of sex.
>
> Eric was angry. He felt he had been promised a great prize if he waited and "kissed dating goodbye." But the prize was nowhere in sight.[15]

This young couple had faithfully followed what seemed to be ultra-wise advice by refraining from all physical affection until their wedding

---

14. Associated Press, "Hazing Death: Too Much Water," CBS News, February 4, 2005, https://www.cbsnews.com/news/hazing-death-too-much-water/; CBS/AP, "Georgia Teen Dies from Drinking Too Much Water, Gatorade," CBS News, August 12, 2014, https://www.cbsnews.com/news/georgia-teen-dies-from-drinking-too-much-water-gatorade/.
15. Irwin, "Marriage and Sexual Wholeness."

night. Four years later, Wendy and Eric had still not consummated their marriage and Wendy was content living as platonic roommates. This is a perfect model of how harsh, overly conservative religious rules often backfire, creating a bigger mess than the one they were trying to prevent. Think of it this way: if a female's biggest sex organ is her brain, and we steep a young girl's minds into believing that good girls shouldn't think about sex and that physical affection is wrong, we are in essence raising female eunuchs. Wendy's God-given sexual desire for her husband was aborted before it had a chance to develop into maturity.

The recent purity movement insinuated in Irwin's article is a perfect example of the legalism Paul warned us about: "'Do not handle! Do not taste! Do not touch!' These [rules] are all destined to perish with use, because they are based on human commands and teachings. Such regulations indeed have an appearance of wisdom, with their self-imposed worship, their false humility, and their harsh treatment of the body but they lack any value in restraining sensual indulgence" (Colossians 2:21–23).

In other words, scripture clearly states that abstinence before marriage is God's will for us. But, nowhere does it tell us, "Do not hold hands. Do not embrace. Do not kiss." That's where the purity movement overstretched their authority. It's not our job to "add" more rules; it's up to us to practice personal wisdom and self-restraint.

Furthermore, nowhere does scripture promise that if we practice abstinence we will mechanically flip an imaginary switch on our wedding night and by *supernatural osmosis* know what we are supposed to think, feel, and do. Neither does it promise that God will shower our marriage with unbridled ecstasy. That's ridiculous.

Yet, for generations, we have passed these unsubstantiated promises down despite the fact that time and time again, uneducated, naive brides and grooms consistently describe their consummation experience as "repulsive," "nightmare" and "disappointing." Sadly, this is more common than we'd like to admit. Motivational speaker and author, Rachel Hollis, in her book *Girl, Wash Your Face*, put it this way: "I was raised to be this good Christian girl. Now I was supposed to be a sex kitten, but had no idea how."[16]

Therese Oneill, in her New York Times Bestseller, *Unmentionable,* writes, "John Harvey Kellogg, one of the most famous physicians of the late nineteenth century . . . was surprisingly sympathetic to the bride. 'Should this night be ugly,' he warns the grooms, 'so shall be the rest of your married life.'"[17]

When we teach our teens to drive, most parents have enough common sense not to hand over the car keys on their sixteenth birthday. (Thankfully our laws require a full year of training.) Most of us are smart enough to realize that without proper instruction our child will undoubtedly suffer serious injury or possibly death. If they survive, they'll likely be traumatized of driving for the rest of their life. If we understand this principle in other areas of life, why do we fail to apply it in matters such as sex and marriage? I'll tell you why. Because we perpetuate what our parents did to us, or rather, what they didn't do. And for most of us, they did nothing. Zilch. Zero. Nada.

I believe what is about to be revealed within the Song of Solomon will give us everything we need to make a healthy, radical turn from these backwoods mindsets. I'm convinced that this interpretation of the Song—though not perfect by any means—is at least close to what the Israelites understood three thousand years ago. Get ready to embark on the Shulammite's remarkable story of love, purity, sexual joy, heartbreak, and forgiveness.

---

16. Rachel Hollis, *Girl, Wash Your Face* (Nashville, TN: Thomas Nelson, 2018), 76.
17. Therese Oneill, *Unmentionable, The Victorian Lady's Guide to Sex, Marriage, and Manners* (New York, NY: Little, Brown, 2016), 145.

CHAPTER THREE

The Song of Solomon: The Opera

The more I study the Song of Solomon, the more I'm convinced that our heavenly Father is a hopeless romantic. He could have chosen to teach us about sex in a cold, scientific, textbook manner. But He didn't. Instead He chose to teach us through a series of romantic love songs—the Song of Solomon. Which says a great deal about His character and married sex. Today we'd probably call the Song an opera or a musical drama. Some might even call it a chick flick.

In God's flawless wisdom, He used poetic imagery, analogies, and metaphors to *veil* the delicate subject matter. The veil was not put there to confuse us. I believe it was put there for two reasons, (1) to give married sex the reverence and sacredness it deserves and (2) to encrypt erotic activity from young eyes until they are mature enough to process it. In Solomon's day, when the time was right, parents unveiled or decoded the Song in a gentle and unembarrassing way—for both the parent and the teen. Let's be honest. How many of you as young teens heard that the Song of Solomon was a book about sex and then immediately went home and tried to read it? I did.

Songs are simply poetry set to music. Poetry is made up of analogies and metaphors that are not usually meant to be taken literally. If we hear an artist on the radio sing, "The sun rose in his eyes" we understand full well that it's impossible for the hot, flaming sun to rise in a person's eye socket. We're intelligent enough to appreciate the lyric is a term of endearment and praise.

Analogies are everywhere, and we use them every day without even thinking about it. At some time or another, in the presence of children or mixed company, we've used the phrase "the birds and the bees" as code for *sex*. Likewise, when the Bible uses phrases such as "he slept with her" (e.g., 2 Samuel 11:4), we adults realize that there's a lot more going on than two people catching some z's.

The Cast

The Shulammite, Solomon's "Beloved"

The identity of Solomon's bride, the Shulammite, has remained a mystery. Yet this ordinary Hebrew country girl captured the heart of the most revered king of all time. She is our protagonist, telling her story in first person. The Song is her anthem. There are many theories as to who this girl might have been, but the strongest contender is Abishag, the young, beautiful Shunammite virgin chosen to care for King David in his final days (1 Kings 1:3-4).

I believe there is a strong probability that the Shulammite and Abishag are the same girl. If I were to make a movie of the Shulammite's story, it would begin with elderly King David tossing and turning all night because he is cold. Someone in his staff suggests they find a beautiful, young virgin to lie beside him to keep him warm. They search Israel's countryside and find the sweet and lovely Abishag and bring her to the palace to care for the frail king.

Day after day Abishag sits quietly in the corner of the king's chambers while David prepares Solomon to take over his throne. Solomon can't help but notice the genuinely affectionate and tender way Abishag cares for his father, and while doing so falls hopelessly in love with the beautiful maiden. She becomes such an endeared and trusted family servant that she is allowed to be present in the midst of highly personal and sensitive interactions inside the king's chambers. In fact, we find Abishag doing just that in 1 Kings 1:15.

In 1 Kings 1:4 we are told in no uncertain terms, that David did not have sex with Abishag. Many speculate that the reason he didn't was because he was too weak or ill.[1] Which may have been the case. Or maybe it was because David knew Solomon was in love with her, and if he slept with her, Solomon would not have been able to take Abishag as his wife after his death (see Leviticus 18:8).

But it's my guess David deliberately identified their relationship as platonic, because in those days it was improper for a man to lie with a virgin before she had been properly trained in the ways of intimacy. (We will learn more about this custom in chapter 6.)

Why then did it matter if she was a virgin? Because only a girl of outstanding character and integrity could serve the king inside the palace. Certainly not one with loose moral standards. Besides, if all they wanted was someone to sleep with the king, David had several beautiful concubines and trained virgins waiting in his harem that would have happily obliged him. For these reasons, I'm wholeheartedly convinced that Abishag was chosen not only because she was a delight to look at, but more importantly, for her nurturing qualities—not for sex (1 Kings 1:2, 4).

---

1. See *Joseph Benson's Commentary of the Old and New Testaments*, 1 Kings 1:4, at StudyLight.org, https://www.studylight.org/commentaries/rbc/1-kings-1.html.

In another twist, Adonijah, Solomon's older half brother approached Queen Bathsheba and requested Abishag as his wife. This might possibly expose a secondary and deeper motive as to why Solomon put his half brother to death (1 Kings 2:13–25).

King Solomon, the Shulammite's "Lover"

Solomon was born of Bathsheba and was the youngest of David's twenty children. Some argue Solomon was as young as twelve when he became king; others say he was as old as nineteen or twenty. However, in 1 Kings 3:7, Solomon refers to himself as "a little child," and the word *child* in Hebrew (*na'ar*) means a boy from infancy to adolescence. Even if Solomon was somewhat older—say, fifteen—when he took the throne, and he reigned forty years (970–931 BC), he would have only been fifty-five years old at the time of his death.

As a child king, Solomon asked God for wisdom to help him govern and rule Israel. Thrilled by his prayer, God decided to make Solomon the wisest and wealthiest man who ever lived. However, wisdom and obedience do not always go hand in hand. In Deuteronomy 17:16–17, kings were specifically warned not to take an overabundance of horses, wives, or gold. Solomon disobeyed all three. Today, we measure military strength by tanks and planes. In Solomon's day, horses and chariots were a king's might. And Solomon amassed a meager twelve thousand horses and fourteen hundred chariots, most of which were imported from Egypt—another royal no-no (1 Kings 10:26, 29).

Solomon also acquired seven hundred wives, but the Bible only tells us of three: Pharaoh's daughter; the Shulammite; and Naamah, an Ammonite (1 Kings 2:13, 22; 3:1; 14:21).

Apparently seven hundred wives wasn't enough, because Solomon decided to add three hundred more concubines to his harem. That's a mind-numbing one thousand sexual partners! So how many hundreds, if not thousands, of children do you think he fathered? That's some daycare. But out of all his offspring, the Bible only tells us of three: two daughters, named Taphath and Basemath (1 Kings 4:11; 4:15); and one son, named Rehoboam, who took the throne after Solomon's death (11:43; 14:21, 2 Chronicles 12:13).

The Daughters of Jerusalem

The Shulammite addresses the Daughters of Jerusalem ten times in eight short chapters of the Song. These girls are her bridesmaids and close friends and confidantes. But more importantly, they are the ones to whom she tells her story.

Why is it so important that we understand who the Daughters of Jerusalem are? The Hebrew explains it better than I ever could. The Hebrew word for *daughter* is *bath* and is a loving address for a daughter, girl, adopted daughter, daughter-in-law, sister, granddaughter, female child, young woman, and here's the one I really love: *a female descendant.* Ladies, this means that we who are in Christ—you and I—who are "Abraham's seed" (Galatians 3:29) are the Daughters of Jerusalem! The Shulammite is sharing her intimate story with *us!*[2]

Who Wrote the Song?

Solomon was a prolific writer and composer. During his lifetime he wrote over a thousand songs, as well as Ecclesiastes and the majority of Proverbs. The opening verse of the Song reads, "Solomon's Song of Songs." So naturally, many assume he wrote the Song of Solomon. However, this does not state that Solomon is the author. It might simply be citing the title of this stage play. It's my opinion the Song was a

2. When the Daughters of Jerusalem speak to the Shulammite they address her as the "most beautiful of women" (Song 1:8; 5:9; 6:1).

collaborative effort between Solomon and his beloved Shulammite. I came to this conclusion based on the following logic:

1. On several occasions, the Shulammite is completely alone, sharing deep, intimate thoughts and dreams with the Daughters of Jerusalem. Who else could possibly know her secret thoughts and dreams other than her?
2. Solomon is never alone, nor does he ever share his innermost thoughts and feelings.
3. Throughout the Song, the Shulammite narrates when Solomon is speaking to her. For instance, in Song 2:10 she says, *"My beloved spoke and said to me . . ."* However, at no time, does Solomon ever quote the Shulammite.
4. As mentioned earlier, the Song is the Shulammite's story in first person. It's her story as an older woman, wife, and mother teaching the younger Daughters of Jerusalem about womanhood.

You may be wondering, *If the Song is a woman-to-woman story, should men read this book?* Absolutely. Why? Because *all* scripture is useful for teaching and instructing (2 Timothy 3:16). Therefore, everyone—including husbands, fathers, and sons—will benefit when they understand the history, customs and metaphors within the Song. In fact, I'm convinced that once men read it, they will be able to see and interpret things from a perspective that I, as a woman, cannot.

Useful Facts about the Song

1. The original Hebrew is one continuous string of words. It contains no punctuation, chapters, or verse numbers. The absence of punctuation makes it difficult to determine where a thought, sentence, or chapter begins or ends.

2. Subtitles such as "Lover," "Beloved" and "Friends" were inserted by the interpreter and not part of the original Hebrew.
3. Jesus said, "The kingdom of heaven is like a king who prepared a wedding banquet for his son." (Matthew 22:2) Fascinatingly, the wedding customs outlined described in the AMEN Theory depict incredibly sound connections to Jesus and the New Testament. In my opinion, far more than any other Old Testament book. Oddly, the New Testament never quotes or refers to the Song.
4. The Hebrew word *dowd* is used thirty-four times in the Song. It is defined by *Strong's Hebrew Dictionary* as "lover" or "beloved." *Genenius' Hebrew-Chaldee Lexicon* translates it as "love between the sexes" or "bed of love."
5. The word for God is not used in English translations of the Song, but God is implied in the Hebrew definitions.
6. Mothers are mentioned three times, but fathers are never mentioned.
7. Most girls reach puberty around ten to twelve years of age. The average bride was only fourteen to sixteen years old. This meant that most girls only had to maintain their virginity for about two to six years. If a girl hadn't landed a husband by the time she was twenty, she was labeled an old maid. This was the standard age for marriage throughout history all the way into the early part of the twentieth century.

Facts versus Theory

Sorting through three thousand years of evolving Middle Eastern wedding customs was daunting and confusing. One reason is because many resources are unclear about *when* these customs took place. It's hard to tell if they go back one thousand years, two thousand years, or three thousand years.

Another reason is because resources often conflict with one another. Here's an example of one of the many contradictions I encountered. Some sources claimed that consummation of the marriage took place at the bridegroom's parents' home; others claimed it was at the bride's parents' home. To determine which was correct, I sifted everything through the historically infallible Word of God. In John 14 Jesus told His disciples, "There is more than enough room in my Father's home . . . I am going to prepare a place for you. When everything is ready, I will come and get you, so that you will always be with me where I am" (vv. 2–3 NLT). The New Testament clearly teaches that the church is the bride and Jesus is the Bridegroom. So, when Jesus says He is going to take us back to the wedding chamber He prepared for us "in [his] Father's home," it makes sense that marriages must have been consummated at the bridegroom's father's home. Conflict settled.

Before we venture back in time on the Shulammite's journey, let me explain how *most* chapters are laid out. The first segment is the portion of *scripture* we will be focusing on and interpreting. The second segment teaches the *history and customs* that relate to that portion of the Song. The third segment is the *Shulammite* or Abi's (short for Abishag) story, retold in modern-day language. Throughout the story you will come across *Unlocking the Past* boxes that illuminate interesting facts, Hebrew definitions, analogies, and metaphors that clarify and decode the Song.

In an attempt to make the Shulammite's story more colorful and realistic, I named some of the characters, added generic scenery and dialogue, and infused a bit of historical fiction.

Lastly, before beginning our story, try to clear your mind of any past lessons or viewpoints you may have of the Song. Inevitably, when I speak, someone will come to me afterward and tell me that she is confused because she was taught thus and such about the Song, and what I said didn't match up with that. I guarantee you, you will be lost if you start this journey with preconceived notions of what you think this book is about.

While I am not seminary trained, I have dug deep in forming my theory, and I have done my best to include all my sources. However, please keep in mind that this is a theory. Theories are plausible explanations using facts and reasonable assumptions. Does it have holes in it? Yes. Do I have all the answers? No. But, I do believe it is by far the most factually-based and logical explanation of the Song to date.

I realize many of the topics outlined in this book may not be popular in certain religious circles. Please hear me. I'm not trying to justify *my* beliefs. In fact, I myself have grappled with some of my findings. I'm simply passing on to you what I have discovered along with my resources.

Come with me now through this intriguing story. Watch as what once made little sense, suddenly make (almost) perfect sense. It's my hope that no matter who you are or what season of life you're in, you'll be able to take something of value from this remarkable story. Because God's Word never returns void (see Isaiah 55:11), I'm convinced the Song has the power to transform and liberate Christian marriages today and in the future. I believe this book is only the tip of the iceberg to deeper insights and endless lessons to come.

 ACT ONE 

Pre-Wedding

CHAPTER FOUR

The Betrothal: Waiting for the Groom

Today, when someone decides to get married, it usually begins with an engagement announcement and a party. During Solomon's day, the first step was the betrothal banquet. Our story begins in Song 1:2 with the Shulammite chatting girl talk with the Daughters of Jerusalem about Solomon, her groom king, while they eagerly wait for him to arrive for the banquet:

[The Shulammite][1]

Let him kiss me with the kisses of his mouth—
for your love is more delightful than wine.
Pleasing is the fragrance of your perfumes;
your name is like perfume poured out.
No wonder the young women love you!
Take me away with you—let us hurry!
Let the king bring me into his chambers.

1. The subheads are mine and not those of either the NIV or BSB quoted text.

[The Daughters of Jerusalem]

We rejoice and delight in you;
we will praise your love more than wine.
How right they are to adore you!

[The Shulammite]

Dark am I, yet lovely,
daughters of Jerusalem,
dark like the tents of Kedar,
like the tent curtains of Solomon.
Do not stare at me because I am dark,
because I am darkened by the sun.
My mother's sons were angry with me
and made me take care of the vineyards;
my own vineyard I had to neglect.
Tell me, you whom I love,
where you graze your flock
and where you rest your sheep at midday.
Why should I be like a veiled woman
beside the flocks of your friends?

[The Daughters of Jerusalem]

If you do not know, most beautiful of women,
follow the tracks of the sheep
and graze your young goats
by the tents of the shepherds.

[Solomon]

I liken you, my darling, to a mare
among Pharaoh's chariot horses.
Your cheeks are beautiful with earrings,
your neck with strings of jewels.
We will make you earrings of gold,
studded with silver.
(Song 1:2–11)

History and Customs

Wedding customs during Old Testament times were of a far more legal nature than they are today. People mistakenly compare betrothal with engagement, yet they are very, very different. Here are some of the ways to tell them apart:

1. Today's marriages generally consist of only *one* ceremony: the wedding. But ancient Middle Eastern marriages were made up of two major ceremonies. It began with the betrothal banquet and ended with the wedding ceremony.
2. Engagements are optional. Betrothals were required.
3. Engagements can last weeks, months, or years, or you can skip it altogether and elope to a Las Vegas chapel. Betrothals lasted a minimum of one year.
4. Today, the wedding ceremony is hosted by the bride's parents. In Solomon's day the betrothal banquet was hosted by the bride's parents, and the wedding ceremony and banquet was hosted by the groom's parents.

5. Today, engagements are a mere verbal promise that can be broken. Ancient betrothals were considered a covenant. Vows were spoken, money exchanged hands, and financial commitments were made. Therefore, breaking a betrothal required a written document of divorce.
6. Engaged couples today are able to see and spend time together. In ancient times, betrothed couples were not permitted to see each other during the year-long period between the betrothal banquet and the wedding. The bride and the groom lived separate and apart, each with their own parents, until the groom returned to take the maiden as his wife (see Deuteronomy 20:7).

The Bride Price

Marriages in Solomon's day were not based solely on the romantic attraction between the bride and groom. They were a legal business transaction between the two families. In those days, a bride didn't just take her husband's last name; she left her family and became an active part of the groom's family and business. People claim that women were bought and paid for like chattel. That's not entirely true. You see, the bride's family would lose their daughter's value as a worker for the rest of her life, but the groom's family would profit from her. To compensate for this financial hardship, the groom and his family paid the bride's family for her value, which is where the term *bride price* originates (see 1 Corinthians 6:19–20).

Brides were expensive. The minimum bride price for a virgin was fifty shekels of silver and twenty-five shekels for a widow. In addition to that, anything of value—land, cattle, servants, or services—could be bartered to compensate the bride's family. Here's the beautiful part that I don't want you to miss: the more a groom was willing to pay for his bride, the more loved and cherished she felt.

> Jacob was in love with Rachel and said [to her father], "I'll work for you seven years in return for your younger daughter Rachel." (Genesis 29:18)

> Saul replied, "Say to David, 'The king wants no other price for the bride than a hundred Philistine foreskins, to take revenge on his enemies.'" (1 Samuel 18:25)

> You [the church] were bought at a price. (1 Corinthians 6:20; 7:23)

> Be shepherds of the church of God, which he [Christ, the bridegroom] purchased with his own blood. (Acts 20:28)

Consequently, if a husband divorced his wife, he was obligated to repay the fifty shekels of silver. And, if he married additional wives without his wife's or her father's consent, he was obligated to pay fifty shekels of silver to his first wife for *each* additional wife he took.

In the event the husband died before they had a son to carry on his name, the wife was obligated to live with her husband's family and marry the next brother in line (Deuteronomy 25:5–10). This explains why Naomi, after the death of her only two sons, gave her daughters-in-law permission to return to their families (Ruth 1:8–9). It also explains why Judah told his daughter-in-law, Tamar, to go back and live with her father until his son, Shelah, reached marrying age (Genesis 38:11).

The *Ketubah*

Once the terms of the marriage were firmly established and agreed upon between the two families, the terms were set forth in a binding legal contract known as the *ketubah*. After the wedding, the bride decorated and embellished her *ketubah*, transforming it into a lovely work of art, and proudly displayed it in a prominent spot in her home.

This custom is still practiced today. Magnificent images of ancient and modern *ketubahs* can easily be found online.

Surprisingly, *ketubahs* are remarkably similar to our prenuptial agreements of today, with one huge exception. The sole purpose of the *ketubah* was to protect the bride—and her only. You see, in Old Testament times, a husband could divorce (or put away) his wife for the pettiest infractions. But it was impossible for a wife to divorce her husband. Nabal and Abigail are a prime example of a woman who was married to a monster, but she was stuck with him till death did they part (1 Samuel 25, Romans 7:2-3).

If you think divorce is devastating to women today, it was catastrophic to women back then. A divorced woman was considered rejected and used property—placing her in a very desperate situation. Much like today, men got bored with their wives, and easily discarded them like trash for trivial reasons, then moved on to a newer model. You see, when Jesus said, "It has been said, 'Anyone who divorces his wife must give her a certificate of divorce. But I tell you that anyone who divorces his wife, except for marital unfaithfulness, causes her to become an adulteress, and anyone who marries the divorced woman commits adultery'" (Matthew 5:31–32). I don't believe Jesus was defining divorce as most people use this verse. He was redefining it.

I'm convinced he was advocating for and protecting wives from abandonment without just cause. He was defending the abuse and cruel treatment of women by raising the requirements for divorce. Remember, until then, the punishment for adultery was *not* divorce—it was death by stoning (Leviticus 20:10).

This *nonchalant* attitude towards divorce is precisely why *ketubahs* were so critical to a bride's future. When a devoted daddy began negotiations with his future son-in-law for his daughter's hand, he did everything within his power to protect his little girl's wishes and future. He left nothing to chance. All major life concerns were spelled out in meticulous detail—food, clothing, conjugal rights, additional wives or concubines, divorce agreements, funeral arrangements (should she die first), and inheritance rights (should he die first) (see Genesis 31:50). A loving father did whatever it took to make divorcing his daughter an arduous, expensive, and painful process.

The Dowry

Many historical sources confuse the bride price with the dowry. The bride price is just what it says it is. The price a groom paid the bride's family for his bride. A *dowry* was what the bride's parents gave their daughter before she left their home and care. It was her inheritance, *not* a wedding gift. Dowries were often a combination of gold and silver coins, fields, cattle, or servants. But here's the thing: because it was *not* a wedding gift, it belonged to the bride, and her alone. It was never to be shared or commingled with her husband's assets. Never. Ever. Furthermore, every item of a bride's dowry was documented in her *ketubah.*

When a loving father of the bride received the bride price, he usually gave all or a large portion of it back to his daughter as part of her dowry. It's said that only stingy, cold-hearted fathers kept the entire bride price for themselves. This explains why Leah and Rachel were so disgusted with their father, Laban, when he stiffed them out of a respectable dowry. I don't blame them for being upset. After all, it was their husband Jacob, who made Laban into a very wealthy man. And the only thing the cheapskate gave his daughters for a dowry was one measly maidservant each (Genesis 31:14–16; 29:24, 29).

Savvy Businesswomen

Contrary to what we've been led to believe about women and finances in the past, the Proverbs 31 wife was a smart, savvy entrepreneur who knew how to manage her money. It's no wonder she wasn't afraid and could laugh at the future. She not only trusted in God's provision, she invested *her money (her dowry)*, into multiple streams of income; i.e., real estate, winemaking, trading, and sewing, and made it grow. As a confident businesswoman, she knew if she ever found herself facing hard times through divorce or the death of her husband, she was quite adept at taking care of herself and her family (Proverbs 31:10–31).

Abi's Story

Now let's delve deep into the Song through the eyes of this lovely, common, Hebrew girl whom we'll call Abi (short for Abishag) in this modern-day retelling of the Song of Solomon.

The year is 968 BC. It's a sweltering August afternoon in the wine country of Israel. Abi's shabby-chic vineyard home is overflowing with grandparents, cousins, and friends who have traveled from as far away as Persia to share in the betrothal festivities. The modest home is crowded and noisy with laughter in anticipation of the arrival of Solomon and his royal procession.

Abi's mother, Becca,[2] a brown-haired, petite spitfire of a woman, is panicking over the last-minute details of her daughter's betrothal banquet. Solomon graciously insisted on gifting Abi's family with everything one could possibly need for an extravagant banquet, but Becca is a proud woman and vows to do her motherly share of hosting her daughter's betrothal banquet.

"The lamb! Has anybody checked on the lamb!" Becca shouts, sticking her head through the kitchen door while fastening a necklace behind her head.

"I checked it just a few minutes ago!" Aunt Lydia, Becca's older, tomboyish sister, assures her. "I've got this covered. Don't worry about

---

2. *Becca* (short for *Rebecca*). Means "beautiful" in Hebrew.

anything except getting yourself ready. We can't have the mother of the bride showing up half-dressed. "

The festivities are scheduled to begin in less than an hour. As the time grows closer, the Israeli commoners jabber on wildly about their expectations of meeting the legendary king of Israel up close and personal. Aunt Lydia declares herself the official lookout and perches on a stool in the front window, peering through the lattice, waiting for Solomon to clear the bend of their lonely country road (see Proverbs 7:6).

"Sound the alert when you see him," Becca hollers across the crowd. "Oh my, if I'm this nervous, can you imagine how nervous my girl must be?"

"Oh, stop worrying." Aunt Lydia laughs. "The king is coming, for one thing, and that's because he is head over heels in love with our precious Abi."

"I know. But I sure hope those brothers of hers are on their best behavior today. If they pull any stunts, I'll . . . I'll personally ring their necks," she bellows back loud enough so they can hear her warning.

"They won't if they know what's good for them!" Lydia agrees loudly with a wink and a nod.

Meanwhile, our giddy, dreamy-eyed bride is sitting down the hall at the foot of her bed, surrounded by a dozen giggling bridesmaids. She babbles on and on about how eager she is to make love to her soon-to-be groom and start their new life together. In her sweet soprano voice, Abi begins her first performance of this musical drama. *"Let him kiss me with his lips, for his love is better than wine. The whiff of his cologne, the sound of his name . . . [sigh]. No wonder the single girls adore him! I can't wait for the King to take me to his chambers and make love to me."*(Song 1:2-4)

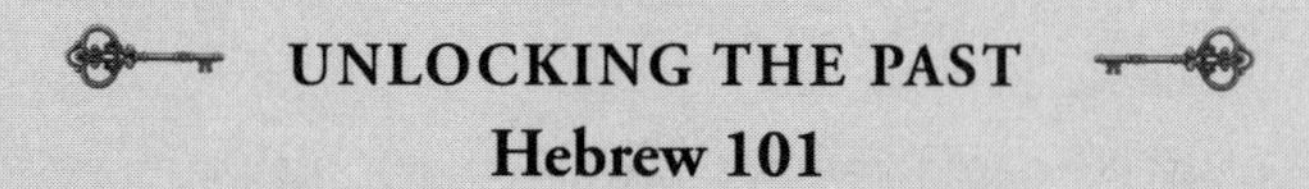

UNLOCKING THE PAST
Hebrew 101

I don't claim to be a Hebrew expert by any stretch. However, many Hebrew experts have attempted to translate the Song with little success, so I will give you my likely flawed interpretation. When I first started studying the Hebrew, I was perplexed because I couldn't find any pronouns. Individual pronouns such as *I, you, him, her, he,* and *she* don't exist. Pronouns were incorporated into verbs and nouns, which may explain why they are translated so inconsistently throughout the Song.

Let's take the first verse and dissect it, so I can illustrate what I'm talking about.

"Let **him** *kiss me with the kisses of* **his** *mouth"* sounds like the Shulammite is talking *about* Solomon. But in the second half of the verse, *"for* **your** *love is more delightful than wine"* sounds like she is talking *to* Solomon. See how the pronouns flip-flop back and forth?

Song 1:2 in Hebrew: *"Nashaq neshiyqah peh dowd towb min yayin."*

Definitions:

nashaq: verb, "to kiss, literally or figuratively"
neshiyqah: noun, "a kiss"
peh: noun, "the mouth"
dowd: noun, "lover or beloved, love between the sexes, bed of love"
towb: adjective, "beautiful, best, better, pleasant, precious"
min: preposition, "above, after, among, at, because of, by, from, then"
yayin: noun, "wine"

See what I mean? All the words are verbs and nouns . . . but not a single pronoun. So how can we tell who the Shulammite is speaking to? Verse 5 states, *"I am dark, yet lovely O'* **Daughters of Jerusalem.**" This clearly indicates that she is talking *to* the Daughters of Jerusalem *about* Solomon. Therefore it would make more sense for the pronouns to be translated like so:

> *Let* **him** *kiss me with the kisses of* **his** *mouth, for* **his** *love is better than wine. Pleasing are the fragrance of* **his** *perfumes;* **his** *name is like perfume poured out. No wonder the young maidens love* **him!** *I can't wait for the king to take me into his chambers.*

Talia, Abi's best friend and maid of honor, interrupts her and hands the half-dressed bride her patina-green linen robe. "Abi, Solomon is going to be here any minute. Don't you think you should stop babbling and finish getting dressed?"

A bit embarrassed that she has lost track of time, Abi giggles and stands up. The girls lift the gown over her head and help her into it.

Her cousin Hadar fastens their great-grandmother's gold and mother-of-pearl necklace around Abi's neck, then hands her the matching earrings to put on herself. Finally, Hadar positions the delicate beaded headdress Aunt Lydia made for her and gently untangles the beads so they hang freely across her brow (see Ezekiel 16:11–12).

"Just think," Hadar exclaims. "When I get betrothed, I'll get to wear these beautiful heirlooms too!"

Another bridesmaid gently strokes Abi's long, dark ringlets. "Your robe and the mother-of-pearl in your necklace set off the green in your eyes. You have to be the most beautiful woman I've ever seen!"

"She's perfect!" Talia exclaimed.

"The king is going to faint when he sees her!" said another.

They stand back, admire her and chant, *"We are going to rejoice and dance in a circle around you.*[3] *Your love for each other is like fine wine. How honorable is your desire for one another!"*(Song 1:4)

The bride-to-be swoons. "Can you believe it? Me, a nobody from Shunem, marrying the king of Israel! Don't wake me up. I don't want this dream to ever end."

Displaying her tanned arms in front of her, Abi whines, *"O Daughters of Jerusalem, I was beautiful, but now my skin is as black as Solomon's curtains*

3. Hebrew is *giyl:* to leap for joy, dance in a circle.

and the tents of Kedar. Don't look at my dark sunburn. My angry half brothers forced me to work in the vineyard, and now I look dreadful!" (Song 1:5-6)

UNLOCKING THE PAST
Angry Brothers

In Song 1:6 the Shulammite complains that her half brothers were angry with her, but leaves us hanging as to why. However, if we look ahead to Song 6:9b, we find a probable motive for their childish behavior. It says that she was "the only daughter of her mother, the *favorite* of the one who bore her" (emphasis added). Nothing spawns jealousy and sibling rivalry quite like being a parent's favorite. Jacob deceived Esau out of his birthright because of it, and Joseph's brothers sold him as a slave because of it (Genesis 25:19–34, 37:3–27). Now, the poor Shulammite is experiencing what it feels like to be the brunt of it.

I'm sure the fact that their sister was about to become the next queen of Israel only antagonized their hatred that much more. As long as the Shulammite was living within their midst, they were going to take every opportunity to make her life as miserable as possible.

"Don't be ridiculous," Hadar encourages her cousin. "You could never be anything but beautiful. And in a few weeks it will all flake off you'll never know it happened."

"I hope so . . ." the bride-to-be says with a pout. "I hope Solomon isn't disappointed when he sees me."

Abruptly changing the subject, Abi asks, *"Tell me, where does the one my heart loves rule the people of Israel*[4] *and rest during the afternoon heat?*[5]

---

4. Song 1:7 This verse is the basis for the shepherd hypothesis mentioned earlier. However, when you understand that the word *graze* is *ra'ah* and means to shepherd, rule, govern, or protect; that *shepherd* is a metaphor for *king* (see Psalms 23:1 NIV Study Bible footnote); and *flock is* a metaphor for *the people of Israel*, you can see that this passage is not referring to a shepherd and fuzzy sheep at all, but the governing king of Israel.
5. *rest:* similar to a *siesta*, a time when people stopped work and rested during the hottest part of the day.

I wouldn't want to be seen near him, or his friends, or for anyone to think I'm a loose woman."(Song 1:7)

UNLOCKING THE PAST
Fatherless

As mentioned earlier, the Shulammite refers to her mother three times in the Song, but never her father, which brings up a puzzling point. The name *Abishag* in Hebrew means "my father is a wanderer or fugitive." That would suggest that the Shulammite's father may have either deserted them and/or passed away before she was born. If so, it would have left Becca a widow and mother of an only daughter, hence obligating her to marry her late husband's brother—subsequently, producing these ornery male offspring. Either way, the Shulammite may never have known her biological father.

They reply, *"Oh, most beautiful of women, if you don't know, just follow in the footsteps*[6] *of the multitudes*[7] *of women who have gone before us. Spend your time with your teenage girlfriends*[8] *at home or at the tabernacle.*[9] (Song 1:8)

"There he is! There he is!"

The girls nearly jump out of their skin as Aunt Lydia's shrill voice pierces through the walls of the house, causing the home to erupt in jubilation. Abi's eyes and mouth pop open. She squeals, "He's here!" She bounds down the hall, pressing through the crowd nearly toppling Aunt Lydia from her stool, and squints through the lattice. Solomon is

6. Hebrew is *ageb:* footsteps or footprints

7. *tso'n:* multitudes.

8. *gediyah:* kids or young **female** goats.

9. *mishkan:* tabernacle or dwelling place.

UNLOCKING THE PAST
Sunburn

In those days "ivory" or creamy-white complexions were the mark of gentility and refinement. Tanned skin was considered unladylike and unsophisticated. We can only speculate how the Shulammite's mean-spirited brothers manipulated her into working in the blazing sun of the vineyard, knowing full well her sunburnt skin would cause intense humiliation at her betrothal banquet.

To comprehend the point the Shulammite was making when she referred to the tents of Kedar, you have to understand that the Kedar nomads were easily distinguished by their black tents, which were made from the hides of their jet-black goats.

leading his long, royal entourage of fluttering purple banners down their country road. With a long sigh she exclaims, "Isn't he magnificent?"

The girls chase after her with high-pitched shrieks and pin her against the window.

"Hurry! Hurry!" her friends urge pointing towards the door. "Go outside and welcome your groom!"

UNLOCKING THE PAST
Canopy Management

One of the most grueling responsibilities of vineyard-keeping was known as *canopy management*. This dreaded task was the non-stop, hand-pruning process that controlled the amount of sunlight and shade the grape clusters received. Too much sun and the grapes scorched; not enough and the grapes stayed wet and rotted from mold. This chore was done every day, all summer long until harvest in late August or September.

Understanding canopy management and the onset of harvest season gives us a fairly accurate indication that this betrothal scene is more than likely taking place in late summer or very early fall.

Abi squeezes through the crowd and out the door, her family following close behind. As the royal caravan creeps to a halt, the crowd swarms it like bees. Solomon slides from the saddle of his chestnut steed and rushes to his beloved. Breathless, he looks into her eyes and exclaims, *"Darling, you are as breathtaking as Pharaoh's chariot mare. Your cheeks . . . your earrings . . . your neck are beautiful with jewels . . . I can't wait to have shimmering strings of gold, studded with silver, made especially for you."*(Song 1:9-11)

UNLOCKING THE PAST
Pharaoh's Horses

Today, the fashion meccas of the world are Paris, London, and New York. During Solomon's time, all the latest and greatest trends came out of Egypt. Pharaoh's chariot mare was a sleek, graceful animal with slender legs and a curvaceous body—making it the epitome of beauty and style. I don't know if it was intentional or a coincidence, but chariot mares were dressed strikingly similar to that of Middle Eastern brides. Both wore elaborate beaded and feathered headdresses and colorful linen robes trimmed with gold and silver coins, ribbons, tassels, and beads.

Telling his bride she looked like a horse was not a *faux pas.* Solomon was smart and charming and knew exactly what he was saying. According to an article by *Scientific Reports*, "Women find men who typically use novel metaphorical language to compliment appearance more attractive than those using prosaic language or complimenting possessions."* And you can bet the Shulammite hung and memorized every word.

*Zhao Gao et al., "Women Prefer Men Who Use Metaphorical Language when Paying Compliments in a Romantic Context," *Scientific Reports* 7 (2017): https://www.nature.com/articles/srep40871.

Taking her hand, Solomon leads his beloved to a white mare draped with soft pink roses and lavender chrysanthemums. After assisting her onto the gentle animal, they ride side by side, leading the royal and ragtag bunch to Shunem's nearby banquet hall.

Befitting a queen, Abi sits straight and elegant. Every time she glances his way, his eyes are fixated on her causing her cheeks to flush. It was obvious to everyone just how love struck the couple was for one another. In a matter of minutes, this young girl would be Solomon's bride—the future queen of Israel. This real-life fairy tale was unfolding before their eyes in this tiny, obscure town of northern Israel.

Making It Relevant

Living Above Reproach

The role of ruler and king would undoubtedly mean that Solomon's duties might require him to be anywhere at any time throughout Israel. As a bride about to go into training and semi-seclusion, the last thing the Shulammite wanted to do was accidentally bump into Solomon or his men. This young lady oozed integrity and being seen around Solomon during her period of separation would have been highly improper. To prevent this, she asked her friends where Solomon spent his time during the day. You see, she had no intentions of pushing the envelope to see what she could get away with. No. She lived by the spirit of Ephesians 5:3, "There shouldn't even be a hint of sexual immorality or of any kind of impurity" (paraphrased). Not a hint, a clue, or an innuendo. Her mission was to live so far above reproach that no one would be able to find anything bad to say about her. Her friends gave her good, solid advice: *Follow the example of older godly women. Play it safe and hang out with us at home or at the temple.*

CHAPTER FIVE

The Betrothal Banquet: The Vows

This segment of the Song is the betrothal banquet. I based this conclusion on three key points:

1. Song 1:12 mentions that "the king was at his table." The "groom's table" was a special table placed at the front of the banquet hall where the *ketubah* was signed before family and friends.
2. Vows were exchanged at the betrothal banquet. Song 1:13–2:3 appears to be a series of short, back-and-forth vows between Solomon and his bride.
3. Song 2:13 states, "He has taken me to the banquet hall." If this doesn't come right out and tell us point-blank that this is a banquet, I don't know what does.

Scripture

[The Shulammite]

While the king was at his table,
my perfume spread its fragrance.
My beloved is to me a sachet of myrrh
resting between my breasts.
My beloved is to me a cluster of henna blossoms
in the vineyards of En Gedi.

[Solomon]

How beautiful you are, my darling!
Oh, how very beautiful!
Your eyes are like doves.

[The Shulammite]

How handsome you are, my beloved!
Oh, how delightful!
[Verdant] is our bed.

[Solomon]

The beams of our house are cedars;
our rafters are fragrant firs.

[The Shulammite]

I am a rose of Sharon,
a lily of the valley.

[Solomon]

Like a lily among the thorns
is my darling among the maidens.

[The Shulammite]

Like an apricot tree among the trees of the forest
is my beloved among the young men.

I delight to sit in his shade,
and his fruit is sweet to my taste.
He has brought me to the [banquet hall],
and his banner over me be love
Sustain me with raisins;
refresh me with apples,
for I am faint with love.
For his left hand is under my head,
and his right arm embraces me.
O' daughters of Jerusalem, I adjure you
by the gazelles and the does of the field:
Do not arouse or awaken love
until the time is right.
(Song 1:12–2:7 BSB)

History and Customs

When the terms of the marriage were agreed upon, they were beautifully inscribed and recorded in the *ketubah.* Once the document was complete, the bride's parents scheduled and hosted the betrothal banquet and ceremony. A large table, known as the *groom's table,* was positioned at the front of the banquet hall. This is where the groom, his bride and their parents sat as the groom read the *ketubah* out loud before the assembly. After the reading, he would pour wine into a cup and offer it to his bride. If she was happy with the marriage arrangements set forth in the *ketubah*, she accepted the cup and drank from it. Then the groom and both sets of parents signed the *ketubah* in the presence of family and friends.

This "drinking wine from the cup" ritual will be repeated once again at the wedding ceremony. In another striking parallel, we find Jesus at the Last Supper with his disciples doing something remarkably similar. "[Jesus] took the cup, and gave thanks, and gave *it* to them, saying, "Drink . . . But I say to you, I will not drink of this fruit of the vine from now on until that day when I drink it new with you in My Father's kingdom." (Luke 22:18; see also Matthew 26:27, 29).

Next, honoring each other above all others, the couple recited their vows to one another. The groom concluded the vows by presenting his bride with a ring or gift of great value, saying, "By this ring [or gift] you are set apart for me, according to the Law of Moses and Israel." This costly keepsake served as a deposit, guaranteeing that he would someday return to take her as his wife. Likewise, 2 Corinthians 1:21–22 states, "He . . . set his seal of ownership on us, and put his Spirit in our hearts as a deposit, guaranteeing what is to come."

At this point, the couple is officially married and aptly referred to as *bride and groom*—not to be confused with *husband and wife.* They won't become husband and wife until the wedding ceremony, which is at least a year away. Some sources contend that the groom then placed a veil on his bride, symbolizing that her beauty was intended for his eyes only. Others allege it represented her faithfulness and submission to him. I don't see why it couldn't be both.

Shortly after the betrothal banquet the groom returned to live with his father, and the bride continued to live with her parents. The couple was not permitted to see each other again until their *undetermined and unknown* wedding day. This is known as the *period of separation*.

Mary and Joseph's Betrothal

The only biblical example of betrothal we have is Mary and Joseph. It's believed that Mary was only fourteen years old when they were betrothed. We have no idea how long the couple was betrothed when the angel Gabriel visited Mary and told her she had been chosen to give birth to the Messiah. It could have been weeks or months into their period of separation. During Gabriel's visit, he also informed Mary of the inconceivable news (pun intended) that her barren and elderly relative, Elizabeth, was also pregnant—six months pregnant.

Needing to see this miracle with her own eyes, Mary *immediately* packed her bags and made the sixty-mile, three-day journey to Elizabeth and Zechariah's secluded, hill-country home. After all, if the angel Gabriel had really visited Elizabeth like he said, and she really was six months pregnant, they were the only people on the entire planet who would believe Mary's outrageous story.

Upon Mary's arrival, she found everything exactly as Gabriel had reported. So, she stayed with Elizabeth and Zechariah for three months. It's my conjecture that Joseph and Mary were betrothed three or four months when Gabriel visited Mary. I believe the Holy Spirit came upon Mary and she conceived shortly after arriving at Elizabeth's. Mary's three-month stay would have put her at the *end* of her first trimester when she returned to Nazareth—right on the verge of showing a baby bump.

Why does this matter? It matters a great deal. You see, Mary and Joseph were practically neighbors in a town of about two hundred people. To protect the validity of the virgin birth and to keep anyone from pointing an accusing finger at Joseph as the baby's father, God put Mary in the middle of nowhere, with a three-day journey and a three-month cushion between her and her groom.

Joseph was no doubt shocked and heartbroken when she returned to Nazareth and heard the news of his bride's scandalous condition. But, apparently he loved Mary very much because rather than having her stoned to death, he decided to give her an inconspicuous divorce. But his plans were bluntly interrupted by a dream instructing him to take his big-bellied bride home to be his wife. Meanwhile, the gossip, as to who the baby's real daddy was, raged on (see Luke 1:26–56).

Veiled Woman: Bride or Prostitute?

In those days, brides wore veils; but so did prostitutes. However, if we do a little digging, it's easy to see there were major differences between the two types of veils. In Song 4:1–4, Solomon described the Shulammite's appearance on their wedding day with the words, *"Your eyes behind your veil are . . ."* and *"your temples behind your veil are . . ."* Then he went on to describe her face and hair in detail. Unless he had X-ray vision, we can logically conclude that her veil must have been made from a sheer transparent fabric. The word for *veil* used in Song 4:3 is *tsammah*, and means "a veil that fastens."

A prostitute's veil however, was just the opposite. Genesis 38:14–15 tells us that Tamar "took off her widow's clothes [and] covered herself with a veil to disguise herself . . . When Judah saw her, he thought she was a prostitute, for she had covered her face." In these verses, the Hebrew word for *veil* is *tsa'iyph* and means "wrapper or shawl." The word for *covered* is *kacah* and means "to conceal for secrecy," and the word for *covered* in verse 15 is *'alaph*, which means "to disguise oneself." These definitions clearly indicate that a prostitute's veil was a large, thick shawl or cloak draped over her head, face, and shoulders for the purpose of hiding her identity.

In Song 1:7, the word the Shulammite uses for *veil* is *'atah* and means "to cover or wrap oneself." Therefore, it's likely implying that she doesn't want to give the impression she is a loose or trashy woman. It stands to reason why any moral young lady wouldn't want to be mistaken for a woman of ill-repute. But what I found ironic is it would have been equally inappropriate for a betrothed bride to be seen in her groom's presence—or the presence of any man, for that matter—during her period of separation. We will learn more about the period of separation in the next chapter.

Abi's Story

The Banquet, the Vows, and the Goodbye

Becca had her heart set on giving her daughter the best betrothal banquet possible. But hosting such an event when your future son-in-law is the king of Israel was beyond intimidating and unnerving. Solomon obviously understood her predicament and refused to let her do it without his help. A week or so before the banquet, Solomon began delivering daily caravans of food, dishware, linens, and servants to assist Abi's family with the expense and work of such an elaborate undertaking. Once his crew arrived on the scene, they worked side by side, in tandem with Becca's wishes.

As the guests file into their familiar, small-town banquet hall, they marvel at the unbelievable transformation inside. Beautiful purple banners flank the walls; long rows of tables are draped with ivory linens lined with greenery, tall gold candelabras, and vases filled with stately purple gladiolas. The room hums with wonder and whispers as servants usher guests to their seats. No one from Shunem has ever witnessed anything of this magnitude.

Finally, Becca and Abi stroll up the center aisle and take their places at the groom's table. Bathsheba and Solomon follow suit. Becca pushes out her chair and stands to open the ceremony. "W-w-w-welcome." Her voice quivers. "Many of you have traveled a great distance in brutal heat to take part in this glorious day. I thank each and every one of you for coming and sharing in our family's happiness." Smiling sweetly and eyes sparkling with pride, she continues. "Inasmuch as my future son-in-law needs no introduction, I present our honored shepherd and king, Solomon."

The cheers and applause rattle the tiny hall.

Becca continues, "And his beautiful mother, our lovely Queen Bathsheba . . ." Another wave of thunderous cheers and applause.

"I'm sure you're all wondering how I pulled off such an elaborate celebration on my modest budget."

Everyone chuckles.

"Please help me give Solomon another round of appreciation for his generous assistance with this magnificent banquet."

Each wave of applause is more enthusiastic than the last.

"I'm not one for being the focus of attention, so let's move along with what we're all here for. Solomon, would you please read my daughter's *ketubah* at this time?" Then, with a modest curtsy, she sits down.

Regal and handsome, Solomon rises from his chair and picks up the *ketubah.* He anxiously clears his throat. "I'd like to thank everyone for the warmth and kindness you have shown my mother and me. It's a great honor to meet my bride's friends and family." Turning and directing his attention toward Becca, he continues. "Thank you, Becca, for hosting this outstanding event. You are a most kind and gracious woman. It's easy to see where your daughter gets her charm, as well as her beauty."

Solomon pauses briefly, gives his bride an adoring glance, then focuses on the *ketubah.* Everyone holds their breath and leans forward to hear the bride price. As he reads, gasps emanate from around the room. Eyes widen and jaws drop in awe at the immense fortune Solomon has paid for his beloved.

As he continues reading, everyone is enthralled by the look of love, gratitude, and intense emotion radiating from Abi's face, knowing her mother will never be in need again.

An opulent gold wine decanter and matching goblet sit in the middle of the groom's table. Those sitting up close notice Solomon's hands tremble as he pours wine into the goblet. Gently he holds it out to his bride. She stands and faces her groom, takes the goblet with both hands, and puts it to her lips. Their faces break into broad smiles and laughter, and the crowd erupts into jubilant cheers.

Each person at the table stands and takes turns signing the *ketubah*. Solomon and his bride join hands, face each other, and sing their vows to one another in a tender duet.

The Vows

Abi: *While the king was at the groom's table, my perfume spread its fragrance. My lover is like a sachet of myrrh resting between my breasts and close to my heart. My lover is like henna blossoms. He has paid a redemptive price for me. He is my En Gedi, a garden oasis in the middle of a parched wasteland.* (Song 1:12-14)

UNLOCKING THE PAST
Myrrh

Other than the three wise men bearing gifts of frankincense and myrrh to baby Jesus, most of us know virtually nothing about myrrh. Myrrh is a thick, sticky sap that oozes from the bark of the genus *Commiphora* tree. The sap solidifies into an amber-colored, rock-hard resin with a rich, earthy aroma.

In those days, women created their own signature fragrances by steeping crushed myrrh, flowers, fruit, and spices in various oils. After several weeks they strained the ingredients from the oil, then took a tiny amount of the left-over ingredients and placed them into a small swatch of fabric, crafting it into a sachet pouch. The sachets were worn on cords around their necks and hung between their breasts. As the heat of their body warmed the sachet, drops of oil trickled down their torsos, intensifying the aroma.

Myrrh had numerous uses, including first aid for cuts, diaper rash, sore gums, fatigue, female issues, the common cold, and leprosy. It was also used as incense and even embalming fluid. As you might expect, a versatile cure-all such as this, made myrrh an expensive, high-demand commodity. No wonder it made such a popular wedding and baby gift.

UNLOCKING THE PAST

Henna

Henna is a thorny bush used as a protective hedge around the perimeter of vineyards to keep hungry wildlife from getting in and eating the grapes. Their deep red blossoms were crushed to make red dye. The Hebrew word for *henna* is *kopher* and is also a figure of speech for *a ransom, redemptive price, or atonement*. The word *henna* in the Song is the same root word used in Isaiah 43:3 for "ransom." "For I am the LORD, your God, the Holy One of Israel, your Savior; I give Egypt for your ransom, Cush and Seba in your stead."

En Gedi

It is believed that En Gedi is the place of refuge and stronghold David fled to when King Saul was trying to kill him.* (1 Samuel 23:9-14) It sits on the western shore of the Dead Sea surrounded by desert wasteland. It's one of only two freshwater springs in the area, making it famous for its lush, tropical oasis and stately palm trees.

*Bibleplaces.com/engedi.

Solomon: *How beautiful you are my darling! Oh, how beautiful! Your eyes behind your veil are like a gentle, faithful dove.* (Song 1:15)

Abi: *O how handsome you are my lover! Oh, how charming. I promise to keep our marriage bed alive and passionate.*[1] (Song 1:16)(We will learn more about the marriage bed in the next chapter.)

Solomon: *I will build our house with beams of cedar and rafters made of grand firs.*(Song 1:17) (We will learn more about the wedding chamber in the next chapter also.)

Abi: *Like a rose of Sharon, I will bear you many children. I am a virgin of the valley.*(Song 2:1)

Solomon: *Like a lily among thorns, is my darling among other women.* (Song 2:2)

---

1. Hebrew is *ra'anan:* fresh, luxuriant, alive, and flourishing

Abi: *My lover is a colorful, fragrant apricot tree among the ordinary trees of the forest.* (Song 2:3)

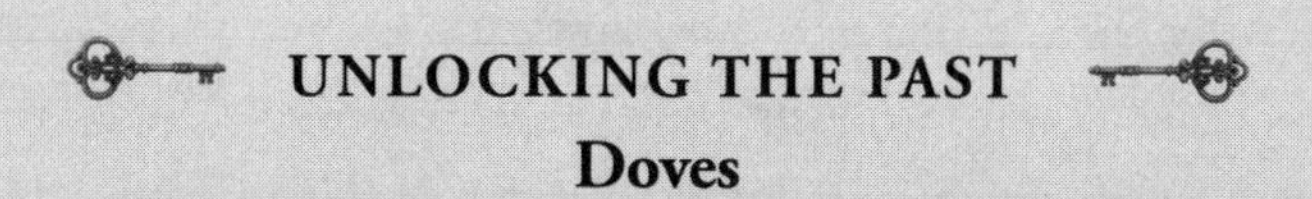

UNLOCKING THE PAST

Doves

Doves are not only lovely, delicate creatures; in Bible times they were revered for their faithfulness, because they have only one mate for life.

Sharon

The Plain of Sharon is located along the Mediterranean coast north of Joppa containing beautiful trees, lush foliage, and acclaimed for its rich, fertile soil.

Hunks and Trees

If I made the statement, "Tim Tebow is a *hunk*," we'd all understand that I was using the word *hunk* as a metaphor for a virile, muscular, handsome young man. The ancient Israelites also had a metaphor for that. It was *tree.* In Song 2:3 the Hebrew word *ets* means "tree," "wood," "stick," "staff," "hard," or "firm."

Let me give you a couple of scriptural examples. Jeremiah 2:20 tells us, "Under every green tree you have lain down as a harlot" (NASB). This passage doesn't mean couples were "doing it" outside under the trees. It's a tactful way of saying that women were behaving like prostitutes and lying under any and every *hard body* they pleased. Isaiah 56:3 states, "Let not the eunuch say, 'Behold, I am a dry tree.'" (LOL!) I think that one pretty much explains itself.

Lastly, Solomon pulls a gorgeous ring studded with emeralds, rubies, and diamonds out of his pocket and slips it on his bride's finger.

Solomon: With this ring, you are set apart for me, according to the Law of Moses and Israel. I promise to return and take you as my wife. Abi bats her eyes in disbelief at the extraordinary piece of jewelry on her hand.

After the vows, the guests are served a feast of tender beef and roasted lamb, colorful fruits, and vegetables of every variety, as well as wine and decadent pastries dripping with cinnamon, cream, and honey. After the meal, one by one, aunts, uncles, and friends visit the groom's table to bestow blessings on the happy couple. Soon, the last few stragglers disappear and Solomon and his bride unexpectedly find themselves unchaperoned and alone in the banquet hall.

Now let's skip ahead. The banquet ended two hours ago and Abi and her girlfriends are once again congregated in her bedroom, but this time the mood is very somber.

Abi is caught up in a whirlwind of bittersweet emotions. She is thrilled that Solomon just publicly proclaimed his undying love for her and made her his bride. But she is also heartbroken because they have just said their tearful goodbyes, and neither of them has any idea how long it will be before they see each other again.

Her friends are trying diligently to cheer her up.

Talia takes hold of Abi's hand and gawks at her ring. "Forgive me, but that is the most unbelievable and pretentious piece of jewelry I have ever laid my eyes on. It must weigh at least a shekel." Everyone giggles.

Hadar echoes, "The entire evening was like that. The whole town will be talking about this day for decades."

Sulking, the new bride stares into space.

Impatient to hear of the couple's goodbye, Talia, blurts out, "You know we're all going to burst if you don't tell us every detail of your goodbye. Did he kiss you?"

"It was an utter nightmare!" The bride gushes. "It will probably go down as the worst goodbye of all time. *I desired*[2] *him intensely and*

---

2. Hebrew is *chamad:* to desire, covet, or lust greatly

wanted to live[3] *with him now. His fruit is sweet to my taste. He took me to the banquet hall and declared his love over me. Bring raisin cakes and apples to renew my strength, for I am grieved*[4] *at his goodbye.*" (Song 2:3b-5)

Taking a deep breath and composing herself, she continued, "After everyone left the banquet hall, we suddenly found ourselves alone . . . He sweetly placed his finger under my chin and lifted my lips to his . . . then he looked in my eyes. *He put his left arm behind my head and his right arm around my waist and pulled my body against his.* My heart pounded in my chest . . . He took my breath away." (Song 2:6a)

UNLOCKING THE PAST
Public Displays of Affection

In Song 2:6 the Shulammite tells her bridesmaids, "He put his left arm behind my head and his right arm around my waist" (paraphrased), unquestionably wrapping her in his arms in a romantic embrace. But, we need to understand that in that culture and time, public displays of affection were considered completely inappropriate for all members of the opposite sex—even husbands and wives. So, the fact Solomon embraced her, indicates they were undoubtedly alone. The only people who could get away with hugging and kissing in public without being frowned upon were brothers and sisters (see Song 8:1).

The girls lean in and hang on her words when suddenly she goes silent, and they notice tears streaming down her cheeks.

"Oh, Abi," Hadar comforts, "Don't cry. You'll be so busy getting ready for the wedding, time will fly by. You'll see."

"I think that is the most romantic thing I've ever heard!" says another. "I hope I find a man who is as crazy about me as Solomon is about you. And as rich too."

---

3. *yashab*: to dwell, live, cohabitate, marry
4. *challah*: to be grieved, sick, or weak

"Abi, please don't leave us hanging . . . Tell us what happened next?" Talia insists.

Wiping her nose, the pining bride continues. "Well, when I felt the warmth and firmness of his body against mine, I melted. Then he kissed me. My desire for him welled up so fast it scared me . . . I was afraid if I didn't get away, I wouldn't be able to stop . . . That I'd do something I'd regret . . . I panicked. I squirmed out of his arms and ran out of the banquet hall. We never said goodbye . . . It was just . . . over!" she wails.

Shaking her head from side to side she eggs them on, "Then guess what happened?"

"What? What?" the girls demand.

"I bolted out of the door so fast, I knocked Gad, Solomon's best man, standing on the other side, into the dirt in front of three other groomsmen!"

The girls shriek with horror and laughter. Even the bride manages a smile.

"Then I hid in the shadows and watched him ride into the hills. I waved until he disappeared into the darkness." With that, she bursts into tears all over again.

"Oh, my . . ." Her best friend exclaims, shoving a kerchief in her face, "That's definitely the most embarrassing goodbye story I've ever heard. But it could have been worse. You could have given in to him. I hope if I'm ever in your shoes, I have the courage to do what you did."

"Yes, yes! You must." Abi straightens up and firmly insists, "*Daughters of Jerusalem, promise*[5] *me together with all young men*[6] *and women*[7] *that you will not flirt or incite*[8] *desire until your wedding night.*"(Song 2:7)

---

5. Hebrew is *shaba:* to promise, swear, take an oath

6. *gazelles:* young men

7. *does*: young girls or maidens

8. *'uwr:* to incite or stir up

Making It Relevant

In today's dating scene, unexpected, hot-blooded moments like this one are going to happen. It's not a matter of if; it's a matter of when. Get your mind prepared and ready in advance what you are going to say and how you're going to handle it.

It would have been so easy for the Shulammite to say, "You know Solomon, technically we're married. Why wait? Besides, who's going to know?" Couples have long justified premarital sex with arguments such as, "Well, we're going to get married anyway" or "We're engaged; what difference does it make?" or "Marriage is just a piece of paper." Not the Shulammite. Had she given in to her passion, she would know, and more importantly, *God* would know. She stood firm in her integrity and made no attempt to water down or rationalize the truth. She did exactly what 1 Corinthians 6:18 (NLT) tells us to do when tempted—RUN! I once heard pastor and author Tony Evans say in a YouTube video, "God doesn't want us to lower our standard. He wants us to grow into His standard." Don't worry about looking stupid or uncool—just run.

The Shulammite repeats this chorus on purity to the Daughters of Jerusalem three times in the Song. I believe that when she said, *"Promise me together with all young men and women,"* she was imploring them to associate and have close, accountable friendships with other like-minded girls and boys. We all need a tight-knit community to help us stand firm through life's hard times. And one of the toughest things we will ever have to say "no" to is the unanticipated downhill spiral of a hot, passionate moment.

Did you notice that the Shulammite also included boys in this pledge? I believe she was imploring her friends that when they entered a new relationship with a beau, to be up front and honest about their convictions of waiting till marriage to have sex. That advice is every bit as pertinent today. Ladies, don't mislead the young men you date or think you can change them. If a boy's convictions are not in alignment with yours, don't waste your time or emotions on him. He is not the man God created for you.

Let me be clear: There is nothing wrong with *feeling* desire. You can still be "pure" and enjoy affection and feel sensual desire. The trick is learning to control your desire and your environment. Think of it like this, if you want to lose weight, you don't stop eating, you control what and how much you eat. The Shulammite wasn't saying "Don't . . . *ever*!" She was saying, "Wait. Wait until your wedding night."

The Shulammite makes an appeal with her friends to establish safe boundaries. Let's face it, one thing sex *requires* is privacy. And one boundary I believe scripture supports is to avoid being in complete privacy with your date—especially if there is access to a couch or bed at night. Look at the trouble being caught alone with Potiphar's wife caused for Joseph in Genesis 39, or David with Bathsheba in 2 Samuel 11, and Tamar with Amnon in 2 Samuel 13.

CHAPTER SIX

The Period of Separation: "When Will My Groom Return?"

As mentioned previously, the bride and groom could not see or speak to each other after the betrothal. This was the period of separation. It was a time of planning, preparing and then waiting for their unknown wedding day and marriage.

Picture this. If the church is the bride and Jesus is the groom, then the church is currently in her period of separation, waiting for Jesus to return. Using today's vernacular, we'd refer to it as "the Rapture." Watch and be utterly amazed at how the following New Testament wedding scriptures seamlessly fill the gaps and mesh with the Song in an unmistakable and prophetic way.

> In My Father's house are many rooms.
> If it were not so, would I have told you that I am going there to prepare a place for you?
> (John 14:2 BSB)

They will see the Son of Man coming on the clouds of heaven,
with power and great glory. And he will send
his angels with a loud trumpet call,
and they will gather his elect from the four winds,
from one end of the heavens to the other . . .
No one knows about that day or hour, not even the angels
in heaven, nor the Son, but only the Father . . .
Therefore keep watch, because you do not
know the day or the hour.
(Matthew 24:30–31, 36; 25:13)

For the Lord himself will come down from heaven,
with a loud command, with the voice of the arch-
angel and with the trumpet call of God,
and the dead in Christ will rise first.
After that, we who are still alive and are left
will be caught up together with them in the
clouds to meet the Lord in the air.
And so we will be with the Lord forever.
(1 Thessalonians 4:16-17)

The kingdom of heaven is like a king who prepared a wedding
banquet for his son. He sent his servants to those who
had been invited to the banquet to tell them to come,
but they refused to come.
Then he sent some more servants and said,
'Tell those who have been invited that I have prepared my
dinner: My oxen and fattened cattle have been butchered,
and everything is ready.
Come to the wedding banquet."
(Matthew 22:2–4)

Jesus replied: "A man was giving a big dinner,
and he invited many;
and at the dinner hour he sent his slave to say to those who
had been invited, 'Come; for everything is ready now.'
(Luke 14:16–17)

History and Customs

The period of separation was a busy time for the bride, the groom, and their families. The groom's side could take as much time as they needed to prepare, but the bride's side was under a time crunch, as they only had one year to get everything done. Once all the arrangements were complete, they had to sit around and wait in a constant state of readiness for the groom's unknown return.

The parable of the ten virgins (Matthew 25:1–13) makes it very clear that the groom's arrival will come at a time when we least expect it and that we must keep our lamps trimmed and ready with enough oil to make the entire journey.

The Wedding Chamber

The groom's biggest responsibility during the period of separation was to build his bride a beautiful wedding chamber for them to live in. Wedding chambers consisted of one or more rooms added to, or near his father's home. This home was expected to be bigger and more luxurious than the house the bride was accustomed to.

Because the wedding chamber was built on and became part of his father's estate, everything had to meet his father's high standards and specifications. Subpar work was not tolerated. Bottom line, the father of the groom would not give his son a certificate of occupancy until he inspected it and put his stamp of approval on it (see John 14:2).

The Wedding Gown

One of the bride's responsibilities during the period of separation was to make her wedding gown. Ancient Middle Eastern wedding dresses were every bit as extravagant as they are today, if not more so. It was not unusual for a bride's parents to splurge on the finest silks they could afford. The bride, along with the help of her female family and friends, spent countless hours not only making her gown, but embroidering it with beads and shimmering gold thread (see Psalm 45:13-14).

The Facts of Life

During the yearlong period of separation, the bride's mother put her daughter through what I call a "maturity makeover." The bride's mother had the responsibility of nurturing her young, naïve daughter into a mature woman and wife. I'm not talking about housekeeping chores, like cooking and cleaning. Girls took an active part in those duties at a very early age. I'm not talking about learning to respect our husbands. That would have been learned by watching her mother interact with her father. Mothers took this time to teach their daughters about her body, a man's body, arousal, intercourse, and childbirth. By the time the wedding rolled around, her meek little girl would be transformed into a beautiful, godly wife and skillful lover (see Song 8:2).

During this time the bride stopped wearing little-girl clothes and started wearing clothes that made her feel like a beautiful woman and attractive to her husband. She would learn how to apply makeup, style her hair, and use perfumes and massage oils. I've often wondered if *quinceañera*, the Hispanic tradition that celebrates a fifteen-year-old girl's passage from girlhood to mature womanhood, is a remnant or spin-off of this ancient custom.

Think of the period of separation as an intimacy boot camp of sorts, in which young brides were learning about their feminine sexuality and fed vast amounts of titillating information. When you understand this, it makes perfect sense why brides needed to confine their social activity to female circles. You can also see why it would be blatantly irresponsible to tutor a young girl on the anticipation and ecstasies of sexual intimacy, then permit her to spend time with her groom and not be tempted to act on it.

Because of this, when a bride had reason to venture into public, she was expected to distinguish herself as "pledged" by wearing her veil. By doing so, everyone, including men, was aware she was spoken for and kept a courteous distance.

As a side note, and for obvious reasons, if a widow remarried, her betrothal period needn't be a full year (see Ruth 4:13).

A Virgin's One-Year Training

Our only example of a virgin's one-year training period is found in Esther:

> Now when it was each young woman's turn to go before King Ahasuerus [Xerxes], after the end of her twelve months under the regulations for the women—for the days of their beautification were completed as follows: six months with oil of myrrh and six months with [sweet] spices and perfumes and the beauty preparations for women—then the young woman would go before the king in this way: anything that she wanted was given her to take with her from the harem into the king's palace. In the evening she would go in and the next morning she would return to the second harem, to the custody of Shaashgaz, the king's eunuch who was in charge of the concubines.

She would not return to the king unless he delighted in her and she was summoned by name. (Esther 2:12–14 AMP)

This passage is encrypted with innuendos that are not detected in the English translation. Let's take a magnifying glass to key Hebrew words in Esther 2:12 and see what we discover:

- *Young woman* is *na'arah*: "maiden of marriageable age."
- *To go before* is *naga'*: "to touch" or a euphemism meaning "to lie with a woman."
- *Regulation* is *dath*: an edict, decree, statute, or commandment.
- *Women* is *'ishshah*: all females as a whole.

Translation: Before a girl lay with a man, she was expected to comply with the decree or edict that required all females go through a yearlong training and maturity process.

Combining my research with this passage suggests that it was a well-established Middle Eastern decree that all females, whether pledged to a groom or in a harem hoping to become a concubine, were required to go through a year of education and maturing before they slept with a man.

As I alluded to earlier, I believe that *this* is the reason King David did not sleep with Abishag. David was ill, and her services were needed right away. They simply didn't have the luxury of waiting a year for Abishag to be properly trained. Again, I'm sure David had plenty of lovely, "fully trained" maidens in waiting in his harem who could quickly and easily have been called up to care for him, if that was the only thing they were interested in.

Personal Lubricants

Another interesting and insightful tidbit of information tucked away in this passage is that oil of myrrh, aside from its laundry list of other uses, was also used as a massage oil and *personal lubricant*. Yes, I'm talking about the equivalent of Kama Sutra oil and K-Y Jelly, which leads me to another question. Do you think it's a coincidence that flavored and spiced Kama Sutra oils, which also originated in the ancient Middle East, are almost identical to oil of myrrh?

Makeup

You may be wondering, *Did women really wear makeup back then?* The answer is a resounding yes (see 2 Kings 9:30 and Ezekiel 23:40). Surely we've all seen ancient Egyptian images and statues of both women (and men) wearing flamboyant makeup and sporting heavy eyeliner. Black eyeliner was known as *antimony* or *kohl*. In fact, the name of Job's daughter, Keren-Happuch, actually means "container of antimony or cosmetics" (Job 42:14).

Believe it or not, mineral makeup is not a new concept. According to *Wikipedia*, mineral makeup has been around since 5000 BC. Minerals were crushed and powdered using a cosmetic palette. Cheek and lip stains were made from red natron, ochre, or crushed mulberries; green eye paint was made from malachite; and black kohl (eyeliner) was made from galena or crushed charcoal.[1]

Today's women long for a "sun-kissed, dewy" complexion. But the women of Solomon's day aimed for somewhat of a pale goth look. They applied foundations made from chalk and white lead to get the appearance of "polished ivory or marble" then created contrast with rosy lips, cheeks, and dark, alluring eyes.

---

1. Wikipedia, s.v. "beauty and cosmetics in ancient Egypt," accessed June 19, 2020, https://en.wikipedia.org/wiki/Beauty_and_cosmetics_in_ancient_Egypt. HistoryofCosmetics.net/cosmetics-history/ancient-egypt-cosmetics/

The Marriage Bed

For decades, I assumed the phrase "marriage bed" in Hebrews 13:4 was a general term used to convey the sanctity of sex within marriage. But my research revealed so much more. When I looked up the word *bed* in Hebrew I found that it is *'eres* and means "a couch or bed with a canopy, covered with hanging curtains." I discovered that the *marriage bed* wasn't just a term; it was an actual piece of furniture. It was an elaborate, canopy-type bed/couch, enclosed with expensive fabrics on the top and all four sides.

Ancient Middle Eastern wedding beds were so grand and lavish it took years for them to be designed and built. In fact, they were such a big deal that wealthy parents began planning and constructing their daughter's bed shortly after her birth. These romantic cocoons were the focal point of every bride's dowry and were given to the bride during the period of separation.

Marriage beds, also called wedding beds, were built on an elevated platform with a mattress designed specifically for lovemaking—no squeaky springs and wobbly headboards. The entire wooden structure, including the headboard, corner posts, and side rails, were carved with intricate birds, bees, flowers, and trees as visual reminders for the couple to keep their love life alive and flourishing. Now let's reflect back to the Shulammite's vow during the betrothal banquet, where she promised Solomon she would keep their bed "verdant" (Song 1:16). It's not by chance the word *verdant* means "alive and flourishing."

Covering the Marriage Bed

Shortly after the betrothal banquet, the bride's parents gave their daughter her new marriage bed, and her mother had the task of teaching her how to use it. Once a bride received her bed, she made "coverings" for it. During hot summer months, thin silks or shears were used, and during the cold winter months, thicker, tapestry-type fabrics were used. The side draperies could be closed for warmth, privacy, and as a barrier against insects.

If you crawled inside a marriage bed, you'd probably be shocked to find amenities such as shelves, drawers, mirrors, and even chamber pots. Another extraordinary feature was the beds were fabricated in sections and put together with interlocking joints. This made it easy for the bride's family to take the bed apart and transport it to her new wedding chamber. Four people, equipped with nothing more than a single mallet, could put it back together in less than an hour.[2]

The Holy of Holies

Old Testament scripture often refers to God as a husband and Israel his wife. In a striking parallel, the Holy of Holies (Most Holy Place in NIV) was a small structure enclosed with draperies or a veil within the innermost chamber of the tabernacle. Now liken that image to the small, drapery-covered marriage bed situated within the innermost room of the wedding chamber.[3*] If that doesn't scream hot and holy, I don't know what does.

---

2. For images of ancient and antique Chinese wedding beds, see Nancy Mitchell, "Five Thousand Years in Bed: A Brief History of Where We Slept," Apartment Therapy, March 8, 2017, https://www.apartmenttherapy.com/a-brief-history-of-the-bed-240124.

3. Hebrew is *cheder*: chamber, innermost part or room

Colorful Linens and Fabrics

In biblical times, poor common folks wore drab colors, such as natural shades of tan and grey. That's because it was very time-consuming and expensive to whiten or dye fabrics. So, the next time you see purple, colorful, or fine white linens mentioned in the Bible, it's a dead giveaway that either the person was wealthy or it was a very special occasion. (Joseph's coat of many colors is another clue as to why Joseph's brothers were jealous of him.) To say a woman wore purple back then is kind of like us saying she wore Versace and carried a Prada handbag. Both allude to a woman of class and wealth. So, when we read that the Proverbs 31 woman wore fine linen and purple, we can confidently assume she was not only elegant, she was prosperous too (see Luke 16:19).

The Adulterous Woman's Marriage Bed

In Proverbs 7 we learn about a foolish young lad who wandered by a brazen wife's home while her husband was away on business. From her front porch she lured him in using the words, *"I have covered my bed with colored linens from Egypt. I have perfumed my bed with myrrh, aloes and cinnamon"* (vv. 16–17). I don't want to waste time on her obvious wantoness. The takeaway I want you to get from this passage is she invited the boy to have sex with her using the words, "I have covered my bed." (Also, did you catch that she covered them with colored linens?)

The Proverbs 31 Woman

No one has ever established if the Proverbs 31 wife was an actual person or an imaginary one. Real or not, she is the model all wives should aspire to be. She was fit and toned, attractive, a supporting wife, a loving mother, an organized housekeeper, a gardener, a cook, a seamstress, a real estate investor, and a philanthropist. Whew! That's a lot to live up to. But, am I the only one who ever wondered, *Why is it, this "perfect" wife, described by a normal hot-blooded husband, fails to list* **great lover** *as one of her esteemed qualities?*

Look again. Now that we understand what covering the marriage bed implies, we can see that it is actually smack-dab in the middle of the passage. Proverbs 31:22 states, "She makes coverings for her bed." I find it pretty amusing that all this time most of us pictured this oh-so-saintly woman stitching custom-made bedspreads, when in reality it means she was gearing up for a romp in the sheets with her man! This was a huge eye-opener for me. Not only did the couple have sex; she planned and initiated it. (You're welcome, men.)

You see, both passages in Proverbs 31 and Proverbs 7 used the same phrase to imply an invitation for sexual activity. In those days "covering the bed" was popular terminology, and everybody understood that. Today, if a cougar told a young man, "I've chilled a bottle of wine and lit candles," he'd get it, and so would we. We would also understand I'm not referring to a large feline.

The Wedding Banquet

The father of the groom had the massive responsibility of hosting the weeklong wedding banquet, complete with an endless buffet of food, wine, music, and dancing. You see, should the father run out of food or wine before the celebration ended it was considered an immense humiliating social debacle (see John 2:1–11).

Invitations to the big day were sent out to all the guests, but here's the catch—there was no date on them (see Luke 14:16–17). Why? Because no one—not even the groom—knew when the wedding would take place (see Matthew 25:1–13; cf. 24:36). It wasn't until the ox and cattle were slaughtered and everything was prepared that the father sent his servants out to notify the guests that it was time to come and celebrate (see Matthew 22:2–4).

All of the following requirements needed to be met before the wedding would come to pass:

- At least one year must have lapsed since the betrothal banquet.
- The bride's family must have received the full bride price.
- The wedding chamber must be move-in ready.
- The wedding banquet must be prepared, and the food and beverage supply amply stocked.

When all these things ultimately came together, the groom's father would go to his son and give him the long-awaited news: "Son, you've done a great job on the wedding chamber. It looks fantastic. The banquet is ready and in order. Your wedding is tomorrow. Gather your groomsmen together and go fetch your bride and carry her away!"

Of course, we must assume that since David, Solomon's father, had passed away, Bathsheba took on the duties and responsibilities of the wedding banquet. I bring this up because David is not mentioned in the Song, but Bathsheba is mentioned on the wedding day in Song 3:11.

Abi's Story

Two days after the betrothal banquet, long before sunrise, the bride and her mother are in the kitchen, packing food, water, and supplies for their last few relatives' journey home. The two women walk them outside and stand in the yard, waving farewell as the first hint of morning light brightens the eastern sky. Abi, obviously glum, mopes back inside and plops down on the living room sofa. With the festivities over and all the guests gone, the house feels cold, still, and empty. She props her chin on the back of the sofa and stares out the window as the fiery sun pierces from behind the hilltop illuminating the sky.

Becca sits down next to her. "My goodness . . . Your eyes . . . Now that it's getting light, you look terrible. You must have cried all night."

"Not all night, but almost," Abi says sheepishly.

"Well, I know just the thing to cheer you up," Becca says brightly.

"What could possibly cheer me up?"

"Close your eyes . . . I'll show you."

Curious, Abi squeezes her eyes shut.

Becca takes her hand and leads her to the back of the house, to a locked, rarely used storeroom. After a long, teasing pause in the hall, her mother unlocks and pushes the squeaky door open. "No cheating," Becca warns, guiding her daughter through the door. Becca stands directly behind her, with her hands on her daughter's shoulders. "Okay. Now you can open your eyes."

Abi gasps in amazement at the lovely, intricately-engraved mahogany canopy bed in front of her. Lying across the mattress are colorful rolls of silks to make bed coverings. She spins around and flings her arms around her mother's neck. "It's . . . it's . . . so beautiful! I didn't expect this so soon."

With their faces only inches apart, Becca whispers, "You're not my little girl anymore. You're a young woman now."

Laughing and crying at the same time, Abi sighs, "I'm . . . I'm . . . speechless. It's breathtaking! It's more beautiful than I ever imagined."

The two stand arm in arm, admiring the beautiful piece. "I'm so pleased you like it," Becca says. "I've been working on it since you were born. You know what this means, don't you?"

"It's time to start my training?"

"Exactly. And we'll start by designing the most magnificent bed coverings Solomon has ever seen. And that won't be an easy task."

That evening, after dinner the ladies sketch multiple bed cover designs. As they draw, they chat about the new wardrobe, makeup, and hairstyles that Abi would like to experiment with as a betrothed woman. The next day they shop at the market and pick out a couple of lovely tunics. Abi tries them on and looks in the mirror. Liking what she sees, she smiles and stands tall. From that moment on she carries herself with an air of confidence and class.

Three months have passed since the betrothal banquet. It's a cool, crisp autumn afternoon. Solomon's palace is enveloped in brilliant red, orange, and gold leaves. The frame of the partially constructed wedding chamber stretches into the bright blue sky. The sound of pounding hammers and sawing wood reverberate across the palace grounds.

Solomon and his chief carpenter meander from room to room through the magnificent open structure, pausing to discuss every detail of its progress. Solomon exclaims, "It must be impeccable. I welcome any ideas or improvements to make it better. I want this to be more beautiful . . . more splendid than anything she could possibly dream of."

The carpenter replies, "I understand. I will do my very best, my lord."

"I trust you will." Solomon nods. "I trust you will."

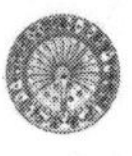

Winter has set in. The vineyard is blanketed in ice and snow. Abi is in her bedroom, sitting in front of her mirror beside a small fireplace. With a tiny brush in hand, she applies kohl eyeliner to her right eye. *Perfect.* she thinks. *Now for the left.*

"Ugh! They don't match!" she fusses out loud.

She adjusts the left eye, then the right, then the left again. "I'm just making a bigger mess," she complains. She gets up and washes her face at the basin, then sits down and tries again and again and again—until her eyes are puffy and bloodshot.

Becca walks in, takes one look at her daughter's exasperated expression, shakes her head, and decides it's time for a different lesson. "I'll be right back." She says and walks out of the room.

A couple minutes later she reappears, carrying a dark wooden chest in her arms. "Come . . . sit with me," Becca invites. She places the heavy chest in the middle of the bed, opens the bronze lock then lifts the lid. Immediately the room is flooded with an enchanting fragrance. Abi sniffs the air, then peeks inside.

The chest is lined with dozens of jars filled with dried flowers, herbs, spices, frankincense, and myrrh. Mother and daughter spread the jars across the bed. Abi reads each one out loud: "Myrrh, cinnamon, vanilla, lemon, hibiscus, rose, coriander, mint . . ."

"What do you say we experiment with your first batch or two of oil of myrrh?" Becca asks.

"That sounds like fun," her daughter chirps. "Besides, my poor eyes need a break."

One by one, Becca explains the benefits of each ingredient and its sensual effect. "Lemon is clean and refreshing. Cinnamon feels warm and tingling on your skin. So what do you think mint does?"

"That's easy. It feels cool."

"Correct. Let's sort through them and create two blends."

Abi and her mother sniff through the assortment, grouping and rearranging different combinations until they settle on two recipes they like best. They put the ingredients in jars with olive oil, coconut oil, and almond oil, then put them on the shelf to steep for a couple of weeks.

Meanwhile, at the palace in Jerusalem, Queen Bathsheba is walking back and forth along the enormous granite table in the banquet hall. The table is laden with dozens of small silver plates, each with petite portions of savory and sweet delicacies for her to sample for the wedding banquet. The head chef, Abbott, a plump, jolly man who obviously loves his occupation, gives a brief description of each dish. The queen begins sampling them, sipping water between each one.

"Oh Abbott! They're all delightful! Every one of them . . ." the queen exclaims. "I don't know how in the world I will make up my mind."

"Thank you, your majesty. I'm pleased that you are pleased," he replies, nodding and grinning.

Abbott makes notes of Bathsheba's choices, then hands her several sheets of paper. "Here is the most up-to-date guest list, your majesty."

She looks it over, scribbles a couple more names on the list, and hands it back. "Thank you, Abbott," she says, smiling. "What would I do without you?"

With a look of admiration, the chef answers, "The pleasure is all mine. This family is my family, and Abi is like a daughter to me. It's my wish to make this banquet my finest accomplishment."

Inside the airy palace stables, Solomon inspects the wedding carriage he has designed for his bride's ride to their wedding ceremony. Master artisans are painstakingly overlaying the intricately carved frame with silver and gold. Sitting in front of the large window, ladies are stitching deep purple fabric and gold cording on the coach settee (see Song 3:9–10).

Overjoyed with its progress, Solomon encourages his team. "It's fabulous!" he says. "Definitely befitting a queen. Keep up the fine work."

Spring has finally arrived. Bright yellow grape blossoms roll up and down the vineyard hillside. Talia, Aunt Lydia, Hadar, Keeva and several bridesmaids have come to get a sneak peek of Abi's gown and to spend the day beading and embroidering it.

Abi dons her pale gold silk gown and playfully saunters from her bedroom, tripping on the long hem. Everyone chuckles at her clumsiness, but the chuckles quickly evolve into oohs and aahs.

Aunt Lydia remarks, "You girls have been busy over the winter!"

"Yes, we have!" Becca answers. "My daughter and I sat by the fire all winter long, needling our fingers to the bone on this work of art."

Her daughter twirls, showing off their handiwork. Becca and Aunt Lydia choke back tears, poking fun at each other's sappiness.

"Ima,[4] please don't start," Abi pleads. "You'll make me cry!"

Dabbing her eyes, Becca says, "All we need is a few minor alterations, and lots and lots of gold thread and beads, and this will be a stunning masterpiece."

"Darling, step up on the stool and hold your arms to your side," Aunt Lydia orders. The bride quickly obeys, and the ladies add a few strategically placed pins.

"Ouch! You got me!" Abi hollers, causing everyone to cackle.

The joyful day flies by and all too soon the ladies leave. The bride and her mother go to the kitchen to start supper.

"We got a lot accomplished on the dress today," Becca says, as she chops carrots.

"We did. The dress is turning out so lovely. It's exquisite even if I say so myself. " Abi lets out a long sigh. "I love you, Ima. Thank you . . . for the gown, the bed . . . you're the best mother a girl could ever ask for."

"I'm just doing what *imas* love to do. I will cherish this time together forever. I pinch myself every day . . ." Her voice breaks, and

---

4. *Ima:* "Mom" in Hebrew.

she shakes her head in wonder. "My daughter is marrying the king . . . It's beyond comprehension."

As they continue to cut cucumbers, potatoes, and carrots, Abi inquires, "Tell me more about my father. Were you happy? I wish I could have known him."

"I wish so too. He was a kind and patient man . . . And handsome too." Becca's tone turns somber. "For the most part, we were very happy. But it was by no means sunshine and roses. He traveled a lot, and that was hard. He died from the fever on one of his trips to Egypt. I was seven months pregnant with you . . . I was devastated.

"I was so happy that you favor him," she continues. "When I look at you, I see him. He would be so proud of you."

After dinner, the two retreat to the back room, but this time Becca is carrying hand drums. She begins to teach her daughter the beginner steps of sensuous dance.

The two women dance for hours, laughing at each other's awkward moves, until tears stream down both their faces.

Howling with laughter, Becca says, "It will feel different when you do it for your husband . . . I promise."

A vicious summer afternoon thunderstorm reverberates through the nearly finished wedding chamber as Solomon and Gad roam its halls. The two men inspect the cedar beams, marble staircase and columns as lightning flashes through the arched windows. "This place is nothing short of spectacular!" Gad remarks.

"Isn't it though?" Solomon nods with approval. "Wait till you see it furnished!"

"You've outdone yourself again, Solomon."

As they stand in the front door, watching the rain blow sideways in sheets, Solomon exclaims, "I cannot wait for Abi to see this place!"

The one-year anniversary of the betrothal banquet is tomorrow. It's another sweltering late-summer day as Abi and her mother pack her dowry, gown, and bed coverings in large trunks.

Closing the trunk lid, Abi states, "Now that we've come to the one-year mark, I don't think I'll be able to eat or sleep wondering when Solomon will return to take me as his wife." Suddenly her lips quiver as she turns to her mother. "Except . . . Except . . . I'm going to miss you like crazy! How am I going to live without you?"

"Don't you worry, sweetheart," Becca says soothingly. "Part of my bride-price negotiation was I'd have my own suite at the palace and I'd be able to come and visit whenever I want. And besides, you'll have so many royal duties you won't have *time* to miss me."

With a mischievous smile, her daughter huffs, "One thing's for certain. I won't miss my brothers a single minute!"

As they fold and pack the last item of clothing, Becca says, "We're almost finished. The only thing left to do is for your uncle to disassemble your bed and pack it up. He promised he'd have that done by tonight."

"Now all we have left to do . . . is wait," Abi sighs.

Fall comes and goes. January passes. Then February . . . March . . . April . . . Every evening before bed, Abi goes to the front window, stares down the dark country road, and asks herself, *Will tonight be the night Solomon returns to take me as his wife?*

Making It Relevant

Maturity Makeover

As you read about the period of separation and what I call the maturity makeover, I hope you've been able to see that, unlike today, young girls back then were not expected to flip a switch and go from "Don't" to "Don't deprive" overnight. They were given at least a year to mature and make that transition. Now that we understand these ancient customs, we need to find ways to modify and integrate them into our modern-day engagement process. We'll need to get resourceful, but it's our responsibility to find ways to foster godly sexuality: mentally, physically, emotionally, and spiritually, in our children and in future generations.

Modern-day engagements tend to be all about the ceremony: the dress, the flowers, the cake, the photographer . . . And that's fun and exciting. But how much sense does it make to have a fairy-tale wedding leading into a nightmare marriage? Like betrothals, engagements should be a time of maturing, learning, and preparing for a lifetime of becoming one. Sex included. The old adage rings true, "If you fail to plan, you plan to fail." Great sex lives are not accomplished by osmosis. Nothing in life is achieved that way. Everything starts with a thought, then a plan, then intentional action. And a great sex life is no different.

Another book I find extremely helpful and informative, to be used in tandem with this book, is *A Celebration of Sex* by Dr. Douglas E. Rosenau. Dr. Rosenau is a licensed psychologist, marriage, and certified sex therapist. He's been a pioneer in Christian sex therapy for over 25 years. His book is an in-depth resource with answers to just about any question parents, counselors, and pastors may encounter on this subject.

The Marriage Bed

For years I was taught that it was the husband's responsibility to create the romantic mood for his wife. But after studying the marriage bed, I really can't find any scriptural evidence to support this. In fact, all the customs surrounding the marriage bed seem to be revealing the exact opposite. I'm now convinced that the reason for this is because a woman's biggest sex organ is her brain. Dr. Kevin Leman, internationally known psychologist, author, TV personality and speaker states in his book *Sheet Music*, "For most men, the greatest enemy of sex is a lack of imagination on the part of their wives . . . I know one young man who said he'd promise to control his thought life, and then asked in return that his wife control her thought life by thinking about sex more. Fantasies about your spouse are entirely appropriate . . . Dream up something that hasn't been done before."[5] You see, the thought and planning process of "covering the marriage bed" and creating a sensuous and romantic atmosphere help women do just that. It helps us get our head in the game.

A Beautiful Bride and Wife

How many times have you heard, "God looks at the heart"? And He does. I'm not disputing that. But ladies, the truth of the matter is our appearance matters to our husbands. John Hagee, senior pastor of Cornerstone Church in San Antonio, Texas, asked the men of his sixteen-thousand-plus congregation, "What are the top ten things you desire in a wife?" Not surprisingly, Hagee reports in his book *What Every Man*

5. Kevin Leman, *Sheet Music: Uncovering the Secrets of Sexual Intimacy in Marriage* (Carol Stream, IL: Tyndale House, 2010), 188.

Wants in a Woman, that a husband's top third longing is . . . "a beautiful wife."[6]

What women sometimes fail to understand is that how we take care of the outside of our body, is largely a direct reflection of what's going on inside our hearts and minds. Let's face it: if we are careless and mediocre in how we take care of our bodies and appearance, then chances are we take care of our homes, cars, and careers the same way. How we do one thing is often how we do everything. Our appearance is a barometer of the degree of respect we have for *ourselves and for our husbands.*

So, be beautiful, inside and out. Your husband will be so grateful.

---

6. John Hagee, *What Every Man Wants in a Woman: 10 Essentials for Growing Deeper in Love* (Lake Mary, FL: Charisma House, 2004), 2.

CHAPTER SEVEN

The Carry: "Behold, the Bridegroom Comes!"

This chapter covers one of the most exciting of my discoveries. If I had been excavating dinosaur bones and suddenly discovered the skull of a Tyrannosaurus rex, it would have clearly identified and confirmed my find. That's how I feel about this chapter. Once you understand the way a carry functions, this segment of the story is not only self-explanatory, it's downright awesome! To me, it's the crown of my research.

Scripture

[The Shulammite]

Listen! My beloved approaches.
Look! Here he comes,
leaping across the mountains,
bounding over the hills.

My beloved is like a gazelle or a young stag.
Look, he stands behind our wall,
gazing through the windows,
peering through the lattice.

My beloved calls to me,

[Solomon]

"Arise, my darling.
Come away with me, my beautiful one.
For now the winter is past;
the rain is over and gone.
The flowers have appeared in the countryside;
the season of singing has come,
and the cooing of turtledoves
is heard in our land.
The fig tree ripens its figs;
the blossoming vines spread their fragrance.
Arise, come away, my darling;
come away with me, my beautiful one."

O my dove in the clefts of the rock,
in the crevices of the cliff,
let me see your face,
let me hear your voice;
for your voice is sweet,
and your countenance is lovely. . . .

Catch for us the foxes—
the little foxes that ruin the vineyards—
for our vineyards are in bloom.

[The Shulammite]

My beloved is mine and I am his;
he pastures his flock among the lilies.
Before the day breaks and shadows flee,
turn to me, my beloved,
and be like a gazelle
or a young stag on the mountains of Bether.
(Song 2:8–17 BSB)

History and Customs

The Carry

Immediately after the father of the groom gave his son the long-awaited news that the wedding banquet was ready and going to happen the following day, the groom had to act quickly. He would promptly notify his groomsmen that tonight was the big night, then arrange a time for them to muster up and set out on their fun-loving midnight "carry." (See Matthew 24:31; 1 Thessalonians 5:2.)

The groomsmen would arrive with an open-air carrying chair, known as a *litter* or *doli,* that the bride would be lifted up and carried back on. A *doli* is a chair with two long poles on each side that extend several feet to the front and back. Men in the front and back of the chair could hold the poles in their hands or prop them on their shoulders. The best man would bring a ram's horn, also known as a *shofar,* and the other groomsmen would carry lit torches.

The strategy of the carry was to get within earshot of the bride's home, just before midnight. As soon as the clock struck twelve, the best man would blow his shofar, and the band of high-spirited hooligans would shout at the top of their lungs, "Here's the bridegroom! Come out to meet him!" (Matthew 25:6.)

The young men continued making a ruckus until they had surrounded the bride's home. Then the groom would stand outside his bride's window and beckon her to wake up and come out so he could "carry" her to their wedding.

The Nighttime Procession

Upon waking up, the bride would come out into the night and they would assist her onto the *doli*. Surrounded by blazing torches, she was lifted up and carried through the town streets amongst repetitive chants of "The bridegroom comes! Come out to meet him!" Then the energetic bunch would make their way to the first bridesmaid's home. Like the bride, she too would wake up, light her lamp, and join the procession. Then they would travel from one bridesmaid's home to another until all the bridesmaids were gathered (see Matthew 25:1, 6–7).

Once the wedding party was assembled, invited guests were allowed to join the procession—but only under one strict condition: no one was permitted to enter the carry without a lit torch or lamp. Not even a bridesmaid. And their lamps had to stay lit the entire journey back to the father of the groom's home. If their lamps went out the Master of the Banquet would not allow them to enter the wedding feast (see Matthew 25:7–13).

As people joined in, the procession would grow into a long, winding, nighttime spectacular. Think Yiddish conga line. In the same way we throw candy and beads today, parade participants often tossed parched grain to children and well-wishers along the route. Many played instruments, while others sang and danced all the way back to the father of the groom's home.

How fun! Wouldn't you love to see a contemporary version of this custom reinvented?

Abi's Story

More than a year and a half has passed since the betrothal banquet. It's a picture-perfect April morning. Israel's landscape is a brilliant Kelly green, with orange, purple, and yellow wildflowers splashed across the countryside.

Shortly after breakfast, Solomon makes his morning rounds through the wedding chamber as the last few accessories are being placed. Maidservants buzz about like bees, mopping, dusting, and polishing every inch.

UNLOCKING THE PAST

How Long Were Solomon and the Shulammite Separated?

Of course, there is no way of knowing exactly how long Solomon and the Shulammite's betrothal lasted. But according to my calculations, the minimum time period was approximately twenty months. Here's how I arrived at that number:

- The betrothal banquet was held shortly after canopy management season, which was late August or September.
- The mandatory, minimum betrothal was one year (or twelve months).
- According to Song 2:11–13 the carry clearly took place in the spring, that is, in April or May. The time lapse between August and April is approximately eight months.
- 12 months + 8 months = 20 months.

Therefore, we can guesstimate that our bride and groom were separated *no fewer* than twenty months. However, depending on the length of time it took Solomon to build the wedding chamber and Bathsheba to prepare the banquet, the carry could have taken place the following spring, or the spring after that, in which case an additional twelve or twenty-four months would be added, making their period of separation thirty-two months (20+12=32) or forty-four months (20+24=44).

It's more impressive than I imagined, Solomon says to himself, gazing up into the looming rafters and engraved marble capitals. With a spring in his step he strolls into the stables to see if the adjustments he requested to the wedding carriage have been made.

Within minutes after Solomon exited the wedding chamber, Bathsheba enters. With her keen eye for detail and design she examines the chamber and is mutually thrilled with its final outcome.

Next, she saunters into the palace galley to see Abbott. As she enters the galley, Abbott smiles and bows. "Good morning, my queen. Allow me to show you through the kitchen and storeroom. I think you will be pleased."

As they stroll from storeroom to storeroom, Bathsheba inspects wooden crates filled with freshly picked fruits stacked on one side, and vegetables stacked on the other. In the next room are large vats of wine and milk, crates of eggs, and buckets of fresh-cut roses, hydrangea, lilies, and orchids waiting to be arranged. "I think we are as ready as we will ever be," Abbott assures her.

Bathsheba lets out a sigh of satisfaction. "You've done a superb job. Let's get this show on the road, shall we? Now I just need to find my son and let him know he's getting married tomorrow!" Turning on her heel, she asks everyone within sight if they've seen Solomon. No one has, so she sets out to find him.

Not surprisingly, she finds him in the stables, sitting inside the glimmering wedding carriage. Climbing in next to him, she gives him a kiss on the cheek and receives one in return.

"Good morning, Ima."

"Good morning," she replies. Then she looks in wonder at the carriage. "Oh!" she says. "The carriage is . . . why, it's simply enchanting."

"Thank you. I can't wait to see Abi in it."

"Well, I just walked through the wedding chamber, and it looks equally magnificent! It's stunning. I'm so proud of you." The queen puts her arm around her son's shoulder. "Your wife is going to be elated with her new home. I also just came from the galley. Abbott assures me the banquet is ready. Your bride will be riding in this carriage . . . tomorrow! *Tonight,* you may go fetch your bride!"

"T-t-tonight? T-t-tomorrow? Uh . . . uh . . . I need to find Gad." Solomon clutches his mother's shoulders and plants a loud, firm smack on her forehead. "I've only got a few hours to get the guys ready!"

Bathsheba tilts her head back and laughs as her dignified king son leaps off the carriage and hurdles onto his nearby steed, spurring it into a full gallop, howling as he goes.

Solomon is dressed, shaved, and pacing the floor an hour before his groomsmen's six o'clock arrival time. It is a cool, clear evening—perfect for a carry. Gad arrives early, holding his family's long, twisted shofar. A few minutes later, the other nine groomsmen show up toting a *doli* decorated with flowers, bells, and colorful ribbon streamers.

After a fair amount of ribbing, the nervous groom and the young men sit down for a hearty meal before their midnight adventure.

While the men eat, Solomon discusses their route and surprise strategy.

"I can picture it now," Gad jests. "Abi and her family waking up . . . running into walls in a panic . . ."

"That's the plan." Solomon laughs, playfully toasting his goblet towards his friend.

The groomsmen walk outside as the last of the sun's rays fade behind the mountain. Gad hands each groomsman a lit torch and a pouch of extra oil; then they enthusiastically set off in the direction of Abi's home.

The men arrive at the far west side of her vineyard about a half hour before midnight. By the light of the full moon, they can easily see her home a little over a mile below.

Sitting atop the vineyard wall, they munch on dried fruit and nuts and sip on water. As they rest, they rehearse their plan of attack one last time.

"It's midnight!" Gad enthusiastically announces. "Your wedding day is here!"

The men quickly top their torches off with oil and begin their descent.

The next musical number of this drama begins with two long, hard blasts of the shofar, followed by Gad's hardy bellow: *"Behold, the bridegroom comes![1] Come out to meet him!"* The men echo Gad's cry in unison, leaping down the hillside toward Abi's home.

Meanwhile, the bride is snuggled in her warm bed, enjoying sweet slumber. Startled by the blare of the shofar, she jolts upright and sings, "*Listen! It's my lover*!" (Song 2:8a) She stumbles across the dark room to her second-story window and spots the tiny torches bobbing across the hillside. Jumping up and down, she shrieks, *"Look! My carry! My lover is like a young stag leaping across the mountains, bounding over the hills!"* (Song 2:9)

Sprinting to her mother's room, she shouts, "Ima, wake up, wake up! It's Solomon! He's here!"

Rubbing the sleep from her eyes, Becca squawks, "Hurry! Go brush your teeth and comb your hair! We'll get your trunks and the marriage bed."

Tripping through the dark house, the bride rushes to her wash basin and does as she was told. Then she applies some makeup and puts on her going-away outfit and veil. All the while she can hear the groomsmen's chorus getting closer and louder.

---

1. Hebrew is *bow*: to carry or fetch

She rushes back to her window and sees Solomon below. "*Look!*" she announces. "*He's behind our wall looking through the windows, peering through the lattice.*"(Song 2:9)

Hoping to get a glimpse of his bride, Solomon presses his face against the lattice and begins his serenade:

> *Wake up beautiful, and come with me. Winter is over. Our time of singing and celebration is here. Wildflowers are blooming. Doves are cooing. The vineyard is blossoming and their scent fills the air. Wake up beautiful, and come with me. My dove, come out of your place of hiding[2] and refuge.[3] Let me see your pretty face and hear your sweet voice.* (Song 2:10-14)

Their separation is finally over! Abi bursts through the front door, and the men erupt in a rowdy cheer. Her mother, uncle, and begrudging half brothers are close behind, lugging her packed trunks and marriage bed and hoisting them onto a nearby wagon.

Solomon and his bride want desperately to embrace and kiss, but they must refrain. He guides his beloved by the hand and assists her onto the *doli*. The groomsmen hold their glowing torches high into the night sky illuminating the area surrounding the *doli*. They lift the bride into the air and begin the procession, Abi's hair and veil blowing in the breeze. Continuing their happy chorus "*The bridegroom comes! Come out to meet him!*" they arrive at Talia's, her maid of honor's, home.

Talia struggles to wake up and staggers outside. Rubbing the sleep from her eyes she holds her torch out and a groomsman ignites hers with his. The next stop is Hadar and Keeva's home, followed by the homes of seven other bridesmaids. Finally, the wedding party is assembled and family and friends are able to light their lamps and fall in line behind

---

2. Hebrew is *chagav*: place of [hiding] or concealment
3. *cela*: stronghold or refuge

them. The convoy winds its way through the streets of Shunem, filling it with light, singing, and laughter, then advances toward the palace.

The jubilant carry pulls into the palace gates at three thirty in the morning. Abi is surprised to see so much activity. Servants run out to greet the exhausted guests and escort them to their lodging for a few hours' rest. Taking advantage of the confusion, Solomon grabs his bride by the arm and tugs her into a nearby room for a stolen moment of privacy.

Pulling her close, he whispers into her hair, "I can't believe this day is finally here. Your perfume sets my senses on fire."

"Oh, Solomon," she exclaims, "you came for me! I was so afraid you wouldn't. I've missed you so much."

Cradling his bride's veiled head in his hands, Solomon smothers her forehead with kisses.

Like most young grooms, Solomon had one thing on his mind—consummation. He leaves his bride with these vital words: *"Get rid of the little foxes or anything that might ruin our first night of passion and hinder our future."*(Song 2:15)

Abi replies, *"You are mine and I am yours. Out of all the virgins*[4] *in your harem, you have chosen me. Our wedding day has dawned, but until the sun sets and the shadows fade, run like a gazelle my lover, put mountains and valleys between us."*[5] (Song 2:16-17)

Solomon places one last tender kiss on her forehead, then backs away and slips out the door.

---

4. Hebrew is *shuwshan:* white flower, metaphor for virgin

5. *bether:* separated or divided by mountains, valleys, clefts, or rugged hills

UNLOCKING THE PAST
Little Foxes

One of the most dreaded enemies of any vineyard keeper was cute, furry, little foxes. Towers, stone walls, and thorny hedges were strategically placed to keep these varmints out. Yet despite all these defenses, these pesky creatures were adept at sneaking in and wiping out entire grape harvests. Once inside, they hid undercover and devoured the tender buds before they had a chance to blossom and produce grapes.

Remember, in Bible times the word *vineyard* was a metaphor for our *bodies*. The word *ruin* in Hebrew is *chabal* and means "to spoil or corrupt," and the word *bloom* signifies sexual passion and desire. Keeping these Hebrew meanings and metaphors in mind, Song 2:15 suddenly takes on an intensely more sexual application than most people realize.

Making It Relevant

Cute Little Foxes

This fox analogy warns us that harmless traits, that sometimes appear virtuous, can actually be devastating to a marriage. What do I mean by that? Foxes are cute, furry creatures. Practically domesticated . . . We might even be tempted to make a pet out of one. But watch out; if you do, it will sooner or later prove disastrous.

Here's the thing. Sometimes what appears to be a friend is actually a foe. You see, we can't be on our guard against something we don't recognize as a threat. In Wendy and Eric's story, the innocuous little foxes they encountered were (erred) religious beliefs, inexperience, ignorance, (misplaced) modesty, and an absence of desire. Some of these qualities appear innocent and maybe even admirable. But don't let them fool you. These traits are a recipe for a disastrous honeymoon, and the ripple effect can last a lifetime. Cute little foxes have been wreaking havoc on marriages for centuries.

Therese Oneill, author of *Unmentionable, The Victorian Lady's Guide to Sex, Marriage, and Manners,* again quotes Dr. Kellogg, "On this subject every woman should have full and reliable information before entering the marriage relation. Mothers should not think that because they were ignorant, their daughters should be equally so. Thousands of women might have saved themselves from life-long suffering had they received the proper instruction at the right time."[6]

Foxes come in all colors, shapes, and sizes. They are persistent, relentless, and will never stop looking for ways to get in and create mayhem in your marriage. In later seasons of life, they may take the role of rearing children, careers, church, hobbies, caring for aging parents, menopause, grandchildren, and on and on it goes. Again, all of these are necessary and noble activities, but if allowed to invade the infrastructure of the marriage, they are harmful. No marriage is immune.

---

6. Therese Oneill, *Unmentionable, The Victorian Lady's Guide to Sex, Marriage, and Manners* (New York, NY: Little, Brown, 2016), 153.

CHAPTER EIGHT

The Wedding Day: "Here Comes the Bride!"

This segment was one of the more perplexing passages of the Song because I could find very little about what happens just prior to the wedding or the wedding ceremony itself. However, I did discover that for the past 5,000 years, it was a common tradition for the bride and the females to get together before the wedding for a *mehndi* or henna party and help the bride get ready for her big day. While there is an abundance of facts surrounding *mehndi* parties, it's difficult to determine which are relevant to Solomon's time period. If this segment is in fact a *mehndi* party, it falls in line with our story, because the Shulammmite is again spending time with and talking to the Daughters of Jerusalem (v. 5). And what do people *love* to talk about at weddings? They love to reminisce about how the bride and groom met, of course. And I believe that is exactly what the Shulammite and her bridesmaids are doing in this scene.

Scripture

[The Shulammite]

On my bed at night
I sought the one I love;
I sought him
but did not find him.
I will arise now and go about the city,
through the streets and squares.
I will seek the one [my heart loves].
So I sought him but did not find him.

I encountered the watchmen on their rounds of the city:
"Have you seen the one [my heart loves]?"
I had just passed them when I found the one [my heart loves].
I held him and would not let go
until I had brought him to my mother's house,
to the chamber of the one who conceived me.

O daughters of Jerusalem, I charge you
by the gazelles and does of the field:
Do not arouse or awaken love
until the time is right.

[The People of Jerusalem]

Who is this coming up from the wilderness
like a column of smoke,
scented with myrrh and frankincense
from all the spices of the merchant?
Behold, it is Solomon's carriage,
escorted by sixty of the mightiest men of Israel.
All are skilled with the sword,

experienced in warfare.
Each has his sword at his side
prepared for the terror of night.

King Solomon has made his carriage
out of the timber of Lebanon.
He has made its posts of silver,
its base of gold, its seat of purple fabric.
Its interior is inlaid with love
by the daughters of Jerusalem.

Come out, O daughters of Zion,
and gaze at King Solomon,
wearing the crown his mother bestowed
on the day of his wedding—
the day of his heart's rejoicing.
(Song 3:1-11 BSB)

History and Customs

Psalm 45 was a song written for King David's wedding, and it displays a powerful image of the gown, the guests, the gifts, and the pomp and pageantry associated with royal weddings during that time. The following segment was written specifically for David's bride:

Kings' daughters are among Your noble ladies;
At Your right hand stands the queen in gold from Ophir.

Hear, O daughter, consider and incline your ear [to my instruction]:
Forget your people and your father's house;

Then the King will desire your beauty;
Because He is your Lord, bow down and honor Him.

The daughter of Tyre will come with a gift;
The rich among the people will seek your favor.

Glorious is the King's daughter within [the palace];
Her robe is interwoven with gold.

She will be brought to the King in embroidered garments;
The virgins, her companions who follow her,
Will be brought to You.

With gladness and rejoicing will they be led;
They will enter into the King's palace. (Psalm 45:9–15 AMP)

The Bride's Day

Some things never change. The wedding day was all about the bride then, and it's all about the bride now. It was her special day to be pampered and spoiled. Brides were not only treated like queens—their gowns and crowns resembled those of a queen. Brides often wore their hair curled or plaited and interwoven with jewels, ribbons, flowers, and beads.

When we think of wedding gowns, we think white lace and satin. But Middle Eastern brides wore brightly colored linens and silks as an expression of their joy. White did not become the trend until 1840, when Queen Victoria wed Prince Albert. The elite quickly followed suit, and Christian churches embraced the concept that brides should wear white as a symbol of their purity.

Mehndi or Henna

Mehndi or henna, is a Middle Eastern form of body art that can be traced as far back as 2100 BC to the Babylonians, Assyrians, and Canaanites. These intricate temporary tattoos are applied on the nails, hands, feet and torso of women and brides. They are made from crushed henna petals, saffron, and turmeric in shades of brown, red, orange and yellow.

The *Mehndi* bridal ceremony was a colorful and joyful all-female event held prior to the wedding. Some historians contend that the groom's initials were camouflaged into the elaborate artwork on the bride's body giving the groom the playful icebreaker of locating them on their wedding night. It is also said that when *mehndi* is applied to the hands and feet of a jittery bride, it has a cooling and calming effect.[1]

Well-preserved bodies dating as far back as five thousand years have been discovered with henna art on them. This tradition is still avidly popular among Hindus, Sikhs, Jews, Muslims, Christians, and Pagans throughout the Middle East, Southern Asia, India, Pakistan, and Northern Africa.

The *Mikvah*

The first task on every bride's wedding-day agenda was to get meticulously clean. But Hebrew brides didn't take one bath—they took two. The first was a head-to-toe scrubbing with oil-and-ash soap in a tub or servant-powered shower. Immediately following the first bath, while still nude and without jewelry, brides immersed themselves in a spiritual cleansing known as a *mikvah.* This was done in a deep pool of water and was a time of relaxation, meditation, and prayer. This ritual is still practiced in conservative and Orthodox Judaism. In the same way baptismals are a core element of church buildings, *mikvah* pools are also a core element of most synagogues.

1. See "Henna," Crystallinks.com, accessed June 19, 2020, https://www.crystalinks.com/henna.html; "Mehndi Ceremony," Cultural India, accessed June 19, 2020, https://www.culturalindia.net/weddings/wedding-rituals/mehndi-ceremony.html.

In another magnificent comparison, the New Testament also instructs Christians, as the bride of Christ, to be immersed in a spiritual cleansing, for the forgiveness of sins in the waters of baptism (Acts 2:38, 22:16).

> And this water symbolizes baptism that now saves you also—not the removal of dirt from the body but the pledge of a clear conscience toward God. It saves you by the resurrection of Jesus Christ. (1 Peter 3:21)

> . . . to make her holy, cleansing her by the washing with water through the word, and to present her to himself as a radiant church, without stain or wrinkle or any other blemish, but holy and blameless. (Ephesians 5:26–27)

After the bride's bath and *mikvah,* her mother and bridesmaids assisted her with many of the same things we do today; makeup, hair, nails, and jewelry. Then they helped her put on her gown, crown, and veil.

The Wedding Procession

Today, brides take a short one-minute stroll down the aisle. Three thousand years ago they were paraded through the town streets to their scenic wedding cite on a beautiful carriage (see Revelation 21:9–10). This grand wedding procession consisted of family and friends carrying colorful banners and smoldering lamps of frankincense and myrrh.

Abi's Story

While Solomon and his bride are stealing kisses in a nearby storage room, Nissa, the thin, silver-haired chambermaid assigned to Abi's care, is outside frantically searching for her. When the couple suddenly appears through the door of the storage room, Nissa is so relieved she pretends to ignore the indiscretion.

"It's a pleasure to meet you, my dear," she says to Abi curtsying respectfully. "I am Nissa, your maidservant. My staff and I have the great honor of helping you and your bridesmaids prepare for the wedding. Allow me to show you to your chamber, so you can get a few hours rest."

"The pleasure is mine, Nissa. Thank you for your assistance," Abi replies graciously. "But I can't imagine how I will possibly sleep a wink tonight."

Carrying a tall lamp, Nissa leads the way through the shadowy corridors to a high-ceilinged chamber. "I anticipated you would need a little help winding down, so I made some hot herb tea and put it on the nightstand. I'll peek in on you after a bit to see if you need anything. Good night, my dear," she says, closing the door.

Abi quickly changes into her nightclothes and crawls into the massive feather-down bed. The warm tea is delicious and soothing and makes her drowsy. Staring through the darkness at the beamed ceiling, she tries to make out the painted murals overhead. Without even realizing it, her eyes grow heavy and she dozes off.

Tap, tap, tap.

Abi's eyes flutter open to the faint sound. She lifts her head and sees her mother peeking around the tall, ornate door. She grins and signals her in.

Becca plants a good-morning kiss on her cheek. "Scoot over. Let me snuggle up next to you," she says, smoothing her daughter's tangles on her forehead.

Soft morning rays filter through the tall, arched windows softly illuminating the spectacular room. Abi muses, "I had the most preposterous dream last night. I dreamt King Solomon came and carried me away and I woke up in the palace!"

Laughing, Becca replies, "That's funny. I had the same dream. It's amazing . . . After all this time I still can't fathom that my daughter is marrying the king of Israel!"

Before her daughter can reply, Aunt Lydia pops her head through the partially open door.

"Look at you two!" Turning to the bride she says, "My goodness! You look exactly like your mother on her wedding day."

Within minutes, all the bridesmaids are piled on the bed, filling the room with chatter and giggles.

Nissa and two younger maidservants roll in carts of luscious breads, fruits, raisin cakes, juices, and teas. Nissa greets the bridal party with a cheery voice. "Good morning, ladies! It looks like this party started without us. I'm sure you're all famished."

"We are," the ladies chime, marveling at the artful display of foods to choose from.

As the ladies cackle on, the bride unassumingly breaks off tiny morsels of fig bread, forcing each bite down with tangy pomegranate juice.

"Darling, you'd better eat," cautions Becca. "You're going to need your strength."

"She's right. You've got a long day ahead of you," Aunt Lydia agrees with a wink. "And a long night too!"

The ladies erupt into a litany of giggles.

Nissa and her staff clear the breakfast leftovers and carts. They return promptly carrying soft robes and slippers made of white Egyptian linen for each girl. Abi's robe however, is stitched with Solomon's royal crest on the left shoulder and the cuffs and hems are scalloped with gold embroidery.

"Come, my dear," Nissa summons. "It's time for you to start getting ready for your groom."

The bride dons her robe and promptly follows Nissa into an amber, marble bathing room with a crackling fire in the corner fireplace. Nissa stands behind a low wall, showering Abi with warm water as she lathers and rinses her body and long dark hair, then pats herself dry.

Nissa then leads her down another series of long corridors to a small hexagon-shaped room, with morning sunshine streaking through the high, arched windows. She signals Abi to enter. In the center of the room is a sparkling blue *mikvah* pool surrounded by dozens of flickering lampstands of various shapes and heights.

"Why . . . why, it's simply magical!" the bride coos.

"Enjoy and take your time, dear. I'll be sitting just outside the door." Handing her a shiny gold bell, Nissa instructs, "Just ring this if you need anything and I'll step inside." She closes the door behind her, leaving Abi to relax, meditate, and pray in the tranquil waters.

Clean, relaxed, and refreshed, Abi returns to the chamber. The bridesmaids are also bathed and eager to begin their beauty treatments. The bride reclines on a couch in the middle of the room. One artisan paints dainty henna butterflies on her hands and nails; another decorates her feet. Becca and the girls sit in a semicircle facing Abi as they, too, have their hair styled and braided. The ladies ponder and babble on and on about their friend's new life as Solomon's queen.

As the conversation evolves, Abi can't help but reminisce about the days before she met Solomon and all the nights she laid in bed, praying to God about the one He had planned for her. Her memories turn to song.

I remember lying on my bed in the middle of the night praying[2] *to God about the one my heart loves—asking Him to help me find*

2. Hebrew is *baqash:* to beg, inquire, or seek the face of, specifically in prayer

him. Then one day, while walking about the streets and plazas, the keeper of the women[3] *saw me and took me to the one my heart loves. Before I knew it, the one I love claimed me for his own. I waited anxiously for the day he would return and carry me from my mother's house,*[4] *the one who conceived me.*

Oh, Daughters of Jerusalem, promise me, with all young men and women that you will not flirt or incite desire until your wedding night. (Song 3:1-5)

UNLOCKING THE PAST
Boyfriend or Fiancé?

Nowadays, while dating, we call our significant other "boyfriend" or "girlfriend." After the engagement, they take on the title of "fiancé" or "fiancée." In Song 1:7, *before* the betrothal banquet, the Shulammite referred to Solomon using the words *nephesh 'ahab,* which is translated "him who my heart or soul loves."

Please note that from the betrothal banquet to the end of the Song, she addressed Solomon as *dowd*, which means "lover" or "beloved," and is translated "love between the sexes" or "bed of love." For this reason, it is my theory that the words "lover" or "beloved" infers "groom" or "husband."

However, in this scene in the Song, the Shulammite switches back to the title "him who my heart loves," which is why I believe she is thinking back in time, *before* their betrothal, when he was still her "boyfriend."

While the *mehndi* on her nails, hands and feet is drying, Abi's hair is styled into a partial up-do with tiny sparkling gems woven into her

3. Hebrew is *shamar:* to guard, protect, and keep. The same Hebrew word is used in Esther 2:8 to describe Hegai the eunuch as "keeper of the women."
4. *"carry from my mother's house"* is *bow' 'em bayith,* the Hebrew phrase for the carry: *(bow':* to come, fetch or carry; *'em:* mother; *bayith:* house).

braids. Her attendant curls the remaining locks and lets them hang in soft ringlets down her back and shoulders.

Once the bridesmaids' hair and makeup are finished, they help each other put on their wedding attire and pin wispy flower wreaths in each other's hair.

"Each of you looks like an angel," Abi admires as her attendant applies scarlet rouge on her cheeks.

"Us? It's *you* who is flawless." Talia praises, causing all eyes to shift to the bride. "Your skin is like ivory and your eyes are captivating."

"Yes, she is," Nissa declares, clasping the sides of her face. "She is utterly stunning!"

"Now it's time . . ." Hadar exclaims, hopping up and down with excitement. "It's time to put on your dress. Come, Keeva. Help me get her gown out of the wardrobe."

The two sisters scamper from the room and return seconds later carefully carrying Abi's wedding dress. They lift the intricately embroidered and beaded gown and the bride slips one arm through then the other. Aunt Lydia takes the matching jeweled sash and fashions it around her waist into a long bow trailing to the floor. Each girl takes turns adorning their friend with bracelets, rings and dangling earrings. Then, Talia hooks Abi's glimmering silver and gold bridal chain around her neck. Lastly, using small jeweled combs, Becca nestles the bride's sparkling crown into her braids and fastens her veil at each temple.

"You are perfect my daughter . . . without blemish or wrinkle. My work is done." Becca says, her voice quivering. "You are ready for your groom."

Gesturing with her hands, Nissa beckons the bride and her friends to a huge, floor-length mirror. "Come and see how beautiful you are my dear. I've known the king since he was a little boy. I have no doubt he will be delighted when he sees you." The girls stand beside her, marveling at her reflection.

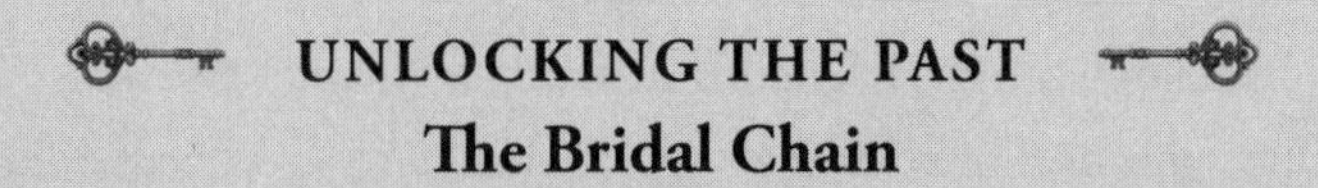

UNLOCKING THE PAST
The Bridal Chain

As mentioned earlier, it was all the rage for brides to wear lots of bling and glittery jewelry. Not only did they wear bracelets, nose rings, earrings, and a sparkling crown; they wore a special necklace known as a bridal chain (see Ezekiel 16:11–13). Bridal chains were fashioned from dozens of shiny coins taken from the bride's dowry. The coins were linked together in long rows and when worn, the coins cascaded down her décolletage.

Some sources contend that the widow's mites in Luke 21:2 were the last two coins she had left from her dowry.

Bam, bam, bam!

Taken aback by the noise, Nissa lurches to answer the door, and two brawny warriors clad in full military uniform step inside. The tallest one announces, "We've come to escort the bride and her court to the wedding procession."

UNLOCKING THE PAST
The Royal Procession

Do you remember all the hype and exhilaration surrounding Lady Diana's royal wedding? More than two million people gathered up and down the streets of London to watch the royal motorcade carry this unknown girl to St. Paul's Cathedral to wed Prince Charles. Seven hundred fifty million more around the globe sat spellbound in front of their television sets.

Don't you know that these ordinary Israelites were every bit as eager and excited to flock to the streets and climb upon their rooftops to witness this fairy-tale wedding? With this image in mind, envision the next musical number as a well-choreographed flash mob on the streets of Jerusalem.

Abi carefully steps forward. The tallest warrior bows and offers his arm to the bride, the other warrior to Becca. The rest of the girls follow single file to the main entrance of the palace.

As they walk through the mammoth, gold-embossed palace doors, they are awestruck at the sight before them. Four white stallions are harnessed to a gold and silver carriage adorned with white, pink, and lavender roses, hydrangea, lilies, and streamers.

"Oh, look!" Keeva leans towards her twin, pointing at the carriage. "The entire carriage is made of gold and silver!"

"It's unbelievable!" Hadar exclaims. "Have you ever seen so many flowers? It even smells divine," she says, inhaling a long whiff.

Aunt Lydia fans her neck feverishly and swoons. "Girls, look at all the handsome hunks in uniform. Maybe you two can snag a couple of them for husbands."

Her daughters roll their eyes.

Family and friends stand in organized groups in front and behind the carriage. Some hold tall, colorful flags and banners adorned with flowers and streamers; others carry shiny gold and silver incense pots hanging from chains.

The two warriors assist Abi into her carriage. Positioning herself in the middle of the purple settee, she sits straight and sophisticated. Then the tall one presents her with a large bouquet of flowers, placing it across her lap. The captain barks a loud command and her heart skips a beat when the carriage suddenly lunges forward.

Clearing the palace gates, she is not prepared for the sight and sounds ahead of her. As far as the eye can see, hordes of well-wishers crowd the streets of Jerusalem. Each person on their toes, stretching their necks to see over the person in front of them. All of them cheering at the top of their lungs, waving kerchiefs, and throwing flowers as she passes.

The wedding carriage is led by a large, colorful ensemble of uniformed musicians. There is a pause in the music, and a lone, husky baritone is heard thundering from the sidewalk, *"Who is this maiden, perfumed with exotic incense and spices; rising from obscurity to steal the heart of the king?"* (Song 3:6) Slightly farther ahead, on the other side of the street, a petite, red-haired woman points down from a rooftop and exclaims in a sharp soprano voice, *"Look! Solomon's carriage, escorted by sixty of Israel's mightiest warriors, each skilled for battle with his sword at his side to protect us from the terrors of the night."* (Song 3:7-8)

Additional voices chime in and multiply from every direction singing, *"King Solomon designed the carriage from the trees of Lebanon. The posts are laid with silver and the base is pure gold. The coach is lovingly sewn with purple fabric by the daughters of Jerusalem.* (Song 3:9-10) Then what seems like the entire city erupts into song, and dozens of vibrantly clad women cascade into the street behind the carriage playing tambourines and dancing.

As townspeople hear the procession approaching, they beckon little girls to come outside and witness what few will get the opportunity to see. *"Come out and follow along. Watch Queen Bathsheba place the wedding wreath on her son's beaming brow. The day his heart is full of joy and gladness."* (Song 3:11)

The merry throng dances and sings as it follows the jubilant procession out of the city gates and up the grassy hillside.

Making It Relevant

The Shulammite's Dream and Prayer

The first time I read Song 3:1, it jumped off the page at me because I remember doing the exact same thing about the same age. I vividly remember at fourteen and fifteen years old, lying on my bed in the middle of the night, gazing out the window into the stars and asking, *"God, who is my husband? Do I know him yet? If not, when will I meet him?"* Doesn't every young girl do this?

Being the hopeless romantic that I am, I believe God has a custom-made spouse for each of us. I'm convinced that if we seek God's direction, then when we meet our special someone, something will ping in our hearts and we'll know, *This is the one I've waited for. The one my heart has been yearning for. The one God created just for me.*

The Bride of Christ: Sexual versus Spiritual

Dozens of biblical parallels can be made between the wedding in the Song and Christians as the bride of Christ. Every girl dreams of the perfect wedding and being the "perfect" bride. But as I studied these parallels, it made me wonder . . .

I've known girls who married to get out from under their parents' control. Women who married because their clocks were ticking and they wanted children. Women who married for money, lifestyle, or citizenship. Some married purely out of physical attraction. Then there are those who marry their best friend and soul mate.

Thinking about the impending wedding and marriage to Christ, our Bridegroom, what is my motivation? Am I merely religious, or am I sold out? I am eagerly awaiting His return and doing all I can to make myself pleasing to Him? Am I learning true intimacy with Him through His Word and prayer? Will I be *ready* when He returns?

Remember in the introduction where I made the nonsensical statement that the Song is *not* a spiritual allegory—yet it is? I hope you are starting to see how it can actually be both a very *sexual* story and a *spiritual* allegory at the same time. The more I've studied the Song, the more I have come to discover an intriguing paradigm and correlation between sexuality and spirituality.

You see, *religion* can be compared to physical sex between a man and a woman who are not in a committed relationship. In other words, they're having sex and living together, but they are not building a life together. The same can be said of our relationship with Christ. Are we just going through the motions of attending church or perhaps even "serving" Him, but not really *knowing* Him?

On the other hand, the personal, vulnerable, and naked *sexual* intimacy between a fully devoted husband and a wife is symbolic of the personal, vulnerable, and naked *spiritual* intimacy Christ longs to have with each of us. This kind of relationship can only happen if we are all-in. Spending time in His Word, in His presence, seeking to love and know Him—not just know *of* Him.

Heaven Rejoices

As a brief side note, I was struck by the way all the citizens of Jerusalem came out to celebrate this royal wedding. In a beautiful parallel, I can picture all the saints who have gone before us, all the heroes of faith, and all the angels (warriors) in heaven singing, dancing, and rejoicing over us at our wedding with Christ.

CHAPTER NINE

The Wedding Ceremony: "You Are So Beautiful!"

Isn't it thrilling to watch these ancient wedding customs effortlessly bring the Song to light? To me it's like owning a locked treasure chest for many years. Then finally, after much effort and determination, the missing combination is discovered and the magnificent and valuable contents inside is at long-last revealed. You had it all along. You just had no idea what was inside or its incredible value.

We are now on the brink of the wedding ceremony, and it will not disappoint.

Chances are, at some time or another; we've all witnessed the intense emotion of a groom standing at the altar, marveling at his bride as she walks down the aisle toward him. The following segment is Solomon coming face-to-face with the Shulammite, and overcome by her beauty. Many husbands will personally relate to this touching scene. Undoubtedly, Solomon's vocabulary will be somewhat peculiar, but nevertheless, his exhilaration and joy shine through loud and clear.

[Solomon]

How beautiful you are, my darling!
How very beautiful!
Your eyes are like doves
behind your veil.
Your hair is like a flock of goats
streaming down Mount Gilead.
Your teeth are like a flock of newly shorn sheep
coming up from the washing;
each has its twin,
and not one of them is lost.
Your lips are like a scarlet ribbon,
and your mouth is lovely.
Your brow behind your veil
is like a slice of pomegranate.
Your neck is like the tower of David,
built with rows of stones;
on it hang a thousand shields,
all of them shields of warriors.
Your breasts are like two fawns,
twins of a gazelle grazing among the lilies.

Before the day breaks and the shadows flee,
I will make my way
to the mountain of myrrh
and to the hill of frankincense.
You are altogether beautiful, my darling;
in you there is no flaw.

Come with me from Lebanon, my bride,
come with me from Lebanon!

Descend from the peak of Amana,
from the summits of Senir and Hermon,
from the dens of the lions,
from the mountains of the leopards.
(Song 4:1–8 BSB)

History and Customs

Resources describing ancient wedding ceremonies have been vague and difficult to obtain. But from the little I have been able to find, I can say with some level of certainty that wedding ceremonies were not religious, nor were they held in a temple or synagogue. Nor were they officiated by a priest or rabbi. In most instances, one of the fathers or an important friend or dignitary had the honor of performing the ceremony.

Weather permitting, most weddings took place at a scenic, outdoor location, such as a waterfall, seashore, or mountainside. After arriving at the picturesque site, the bride presented herself to her groom. Then the head of ceremonies spoke a benediction or blessing over the couple and they exchanged vows again. Lastly, the bride and groom ended the ceremony in the same way they ended the betrothal banquet—each taking a sip of wine from the same cup (see Matthew 26:27-29).

The Groom

In keeping with the royal theme, grooms were also outfitted like kings. They wore flowing robes, an ornamental silk sash around their waist, and lace-up sandals. They also sported liberal amounts of jewelry, including rings, necklaces, and a gold or silver crown or a garland of flowers. Their garments were also perfumed with exotic spices, frankincense, and myrrh.

Abi's Story

While Bathsheba was busy planning the wedding, she knew exactly where she wanted the ceremony to take place—the majestic summit of Amana. It was a spectacular location with a breathtaking view of Mount Lebanon's snow-capped peaks.

UNLOCKING THE PAST
The Crest of Amana

So where did the wedding in the Song take place? I believe it took place on the crest of Amana. Let me explain. The words "coming up" in Song 3:6 in Hebrew is *'alah* and means *to ascend, or climb.* This tells us that the wedding procession is traveling *up.* Up where? Up to the crest of Amana. How do we know this? Because when the ceremony is over, Solomon invites his bride to "*descend* from the crest of Amana" (emphasis added).

The crest of Amana is a summit with a breathtaking view of Mount Lebanon, Israel's highest peak. *Lebanon* means "white" in Hebrew; therefore, it is quite fitting that this mountain, which is crowned with snow year round, be called White Mountain. Wow. What a dramatic backdrop for a royal wedding!

Prior to the wedding, Bathsheba had twelve tall, marble columns erected in the shape of a large square on top of the crest. Invited guests would watch the ceremony inside the square, and bystanders would watch from outside. The morning of the ceremony, Bathsheba had each column topped with lush greenery, flowers, and streamers. Large royal banners were positioned at the entrance into the square.

Somehow Abi took for granted the wedding would be held in Jerusalem's beautiful city square. But as they pass through the square, then the city gates, and towards the hill, it suddenly dawns on her: *Of course! The Crest of Amana. What an exhilarating spot for a wedding!*

As the carriage comes to a halt at the top of the vibrant green summit, Abi gasps in awe at the grand columns and spectacular view. She scours back and forth across the crest in search of Solomon, but he is nowhere in sight. Hordes of people press tightly together outside the columns to watch, many with small children propped on their daddies' shoulders. Family and friends take their place inside the columns.

After several minutes, the head of ceremonies, Solomon, Gad, and the other groomsmen appear and take their stand at the front of the square with their backs to the majestic mountain. Solomon stands tall and regal in his flowing purple robe, but his nerves give him away as he fidgets with his rings and sash.

Gad leans over and whispers, "I've never seen you so nervous and fidgety."

"Is it that obvious?" Solomon mumbles. They both chuckle.

Escorted by a handsome warrior, Bathsheba walks up the aisle and approaches her son, carrying a wreath of flowers in her hands. She carefully places the wreath on Solomon's brow, air kisses each cheek, then takes her seat of honor near the front. Becca is escorted in the same manner and takes her seat next to Bathsheba.

Meanwhile behind the horses and carriage, out of everyone's view, the bridesmaids form a line. The two warriors approach the carriage. Smiling brightly, they stretch out their hands to the bride, "Your Highness, it's time to meet your groom," cautiously supporting her down the steps of the carriage.

As Abi walks past her bridesmaids to take her place at the end of the line, each girl praises and blesses her. She steps behind Talia, her maid of honor, and they softly embrace. One at a time, the bridesmaids step from behind the carriage and promenade through the crowd, standing opposite the groomsmen.

After a brief delay, Abi takes a deep breath and steps out from behind the carriage. Her ankles and knees tremble beneath her gown. Her face flushes as oohs and ahhs rise from the crowd.

The setting sun throws brilliant flashes of light off her beaded gown, bridal chain, and crown. Like a radiant angel, she floats to her groom coming face-to-face with him. Overcome by her beauty, tears fill his eyes, and he sings:

> *How beautiful you are my darling! Oh, how beautiful! Your eyes behind your veil are like doves. Your hair is like shiny, ebony goats descending Mount Gilead. Your smile is as brilliant as newly shorn sheep after washing—not one is missing. Your lips are as lovely as a scarlet ribbon. Your cheeks behind your veil are like the blush of a pomegranate.* (Song 4:1-3)

UNLOCKING THE PAST
Black Goats/White Sheep

I can assure you, the Shulammite wasn't having a baaaad hair day. (Sorry. I couldn't resist.) What seems to be another insolent blunder is another word picture likening her espresso ringlets cascading down her shoulders to the black glistening wool of goats winding down a rocky hillside.

In contrast, freshly shorn sheep were a vibrant white after washing. Therefore, the bride's smile must have been one any dentist or orthodontist would be proud of: bright white, straight, and not a single one missing.

Solomon continues to sing his bride's praises

> *Your neck is slender and elegant like the tower of David. On it hang the shields of a thousand warriors. Your breasts are like soft, untouched twin fawns of a gazelle.*

Our wedding day has dawned, when the shadows flee[1] *we will go to the mountain and hills*[2] *of passion.*[3]

You are beautiful my darling and utterly perfect. Come with me from Lebanon, my young wife.[4] *Come with me from Lebanon. Let us descend the Crest of Amana, the summit of Hermon, past the dwelling place of the lion and the leopard before nightfall.* (Song 4:4-8)

UNLOCKING THE PAST
Cleavage and Fashion Trends

For centuries and in most parts of the world, it was ill-mannered for women to wear low-cut garments in the morning or early afternoon hours. It was however, acceptable to show your décolletage at formal affairs in the late afternoon or evening. Even hard-core Victorian prudes made an exception for this fashion trend.

I was unable to confirm if this custom went as far back as Solomon's day. However, if we consider that the word *breasts* in Song 4:5 comes from the Hebrew word *shad*, which means "bulging female bosom," it seems quite plausible that the Shulammite is showing off a peek of cleavage in this scene.

Now that we've learned what a bridal chain is, it's easy to envision that the *thousand shields* hanging from her neck described in this passage are the many coins that make up her bridal chain.

1. "*the day breaks and shadows flee*": the wedding day from dawn to nightfall
2. "*mountain and hills*": some assume this to be a woman's breasts
3. "*myrrh and frankincense*": symbols of sexual passion
4. Hebrew is *kallah:* young bride, wife, or spouse

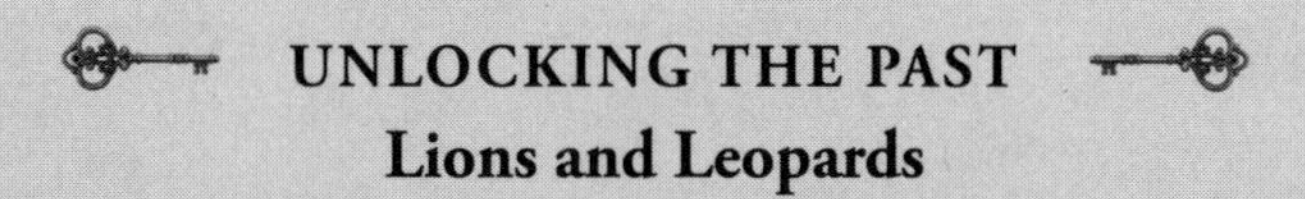

UNLOCKING THE PAST
Lions and Leopards

Lions and leopards are nocturnal animals and come out of their dens to hunt their prey at night. Therefore, as nightfall approaches, Solomon states that they must get out of harms way before hungry felines leave their dens.

The head of ceremonies speaks a final blessing over the couple. Solomon concludes the ceremony by once again pouring wine into a goblet, taking a sip, then offering it to his bride. She sips. The cheers from the crowd are deafening. With sheer bliss on their faces, the newlyweds depart and climb into the wedding carriage together. Guests quickly disperse and begin their descent down the hillside to the wedding banquet. The warriors again take their positions around the carriage as it trails behind the crowd. As the sun sinks behind the jagged peaks, the sky ignites into fiery shades of gold, orange, pink, and purple.

Making It Relevant

You Are Enough

What a grand and exciting celebration! I don't know about you, but I find it encouraging and extremely assuring that Solomon, this larger-than-life king, could be so hopelessly love struck with this unknown country girl. And he was not in the least bit hesitant to broadcast and display his love for her in front of the world. Unlike a political wife, she was loved for who she was. Not for her family, her status, or what she could do for Solomon.

We, too, are loved for who we are. Our Bridegroom—our King—loves us with all His heart. He loves you for you, and He loves me for me. Bask in that thought.

CHAPTER TEN

The Wedding Night: Consummation

READER DISCRETION IS ADVISED: The following content is mature subject matter and intended for engaged, married, or sexually mature couples and adults.

The ancient customs surrounding consummation were such a drastic contrast to our modern-day, Western, Christian culture, I found them absolutely alarming. That's why it's so important we remind ourselves that to the people of that era, the wedding tradition you are about to discover, was entirely familiar and routine.

You see, back then consummation was the final *physical* vow the bride and groom made with each other ***before*** the two were considered "one." And consummation had to take place *before* the banquet could begin. This chapter is the intensely erotic consummation scene between the Shulammite and Solomon. God has tastefully veiled the graphic content behind Hebrew metaphors and analogies. Therefore, in order to understand the fullness of what is taking place, I highly recommend you read the numerous Hebrew definitions provided in the footnotes.

Scripture

[Solomon]

You have captured my heart,
my sister, my bride;
you have stolen my heart with one glance of your eyes,
with one jewel of your neck.
How delightful is your love,
my sister, my bride!
Your love is much better than wine,
and the fragrance of your perfume than all spices.
Your lips, my bride,
drip sweetness like the honeycomb;
honey and milk are under your tongue,
and the fragrance of your garments
is like the aroma of Lebanon.

My sister, my bride, you are a garden locked up,
a spring enclosed, a fountain sealed.
Your branches are an orchard of pomegranates
with the choicest of fruits, with henna and nard,
with nard and saffron, calamus and cinnamon,
with every kind of frankincense tree,
with myrrh and aloes,
with all the finest spices.

You are a garden spring,
a well of fresh water
flowing down from Lebanon.

[The Shulammite]

Awake, O north wind,
and come, O south wind.
Breathe on my garden,
and spread the fragrance of its spices.
Let my beloved come into his garden
and taste its choicest fruits.

[Solomon]

I have come to my garden, my sister, my bride;
I have gathered my myrrh with my spice.
I have eaten my honeycomb with my honey;
I have drunk my wine with my milk.

[The Master of the Banquet]

Eat, O friends, and drink;
drink freely, O beloved.
(Song 4:9–5:1 BSB)

History and Customs

The Virginity Cloth

Another of the bride's many duties during the period of separation was to make a virginity cloth for their wedding night. Virginity cloths were generally about two feet square, and the couple's names were embroidered on it. It was placed on the marriage bed, and the couple consummated the marriage on top of it, capturing the bride's blood, mingled with the groom's semen.

This piece of fabric not only served as proof of their physical union, it also served as a legal document validating the bride's virginity. The cloth was held and safeguarded by the bride's parents in the unlikely event their daughter's virtue was ever challenged (see Deuteronomy 22:13–21).

Consummation

Today newlyweds sneak away to an isolated tropical island, secluded mountain cabin or cruise and consummate their marriage *after* the wedding and reception. However, in Old Testament days, the marriage was consummated *immediately* after the ceremony but *before* the banquet. The couple spent their first week as husband and wife celebrating their banquet with family and friends.

Here's how it played out: After the ceremony all the invited guests went back to the father's house to attend the banquet. Shortly after everyone arrived, the groom would take hold of the corner hem of his robe and place it over his bride's head. This gesture indicated it was time to enter the wedding chamber (see Ruth 3:9–10; Ezekiel 16:8). The groom then took his bride into the wedding chamber while both sets of parents and the wedding party waited outside their door as witnesses to the sacred event.

While consummation was taking place, guests waited patiently twiddling their thumbs. There was no such thing as cocktail hour. Food and wine could not be served until the holy act was complete. The groom then took the bloodstained virginity cloth to the door of the wedding chamber and displayed it to the witnesses waiting outside, formally announcing that the marriage was complete.

It wasn't until then that the master of the banquet could announce to his throng of thirsty, hungry guests that the festivities could begin.

Everyone cheered, the buffet and the bar were opened, and music and dancing ensued.

The Wedding Banquet

The only royal banquet I could find in the Old Testament is in Esther 1, and the visuals provided are extremely informative and realistic. In this scene we find King Xerxes throwing a lavish, seven-day banquet for his political dignitaries.

> The king held a banquet for all the people who were present at the citadel in Susa [the capital], from the greatest [in importance] to the least, a seven-day feast in the courtyard of the garden of the king's palace. There were curtains (draperies) of fine white and violet linen fastened with cords of fine purple linen to silver rings and marble columns. The couches of gold and silver rested on a mosaic floor of porphyry, marble, mother-of-pearl, and precious colored stones. Drinks were served in various kinds of golden goblets, and the royal wine was plentiful, in accordance with the generosity of the king. (Esther 1:5–7 AMP)

This is an amazing word picture and sounds like a party we wouldn't want to miss. However, keep in mind that Solomon was notorious for doing everything bigger, better, and badder than anyone else. So there's a good chance that King Xerxes's banquet looked like an outdoor barbecue compared to Solomon's wedding banquet.

Wedding Garments

Little is known about wedding garments; however, most scholars believe they were provided by the father of the groom, and all the guests were required to wear them. Refusal to comply was a grave insult to the host. In Matthew 22, Jesus tells the story of a guest who attended a wedding banquet but failed to wear the wedding clothes given to him by the master. The belligerent guest was swiftly bounced out of the festivities and the gates locked behind him.

Abi's Story

After the ceremony, the newlyweds delight in the spectacular sunset as they ride down the hillside. As the "shadows flee" into darkness both are hyper aware and excited for the life-changing event that will soon take place.

Long lines form at the palace gates as servants hand out white linen garments to each guest. They promptly put them on then gather down both sides of the stone driveway to hail in the new bride and groom. When the carriage pulls through the heavy gates the roar of the crowd can be heard for miles.

"See!" Solomon says with an endearing smile "They love you already."

"Oh, Solomon, it's like a dream. It's . . . it's magical," the blushing bride squeals as they enter the grounds. Pointing she shouts, "Oh look! Look at all the beautiful lanterns. They look like stars!"

"Yes, they do!" Solomon says, bobbing his head. "Leave it to my mother; she definitely knows how to throw a party."

The carriage comes to a slow halt at the entrance of the courtyard and the crowd engulfs it. The palace is decorated in unprecedented splendor. Flower arrangements hang like massive palm fronds from the top of ivory columns. Purple linen draperies flank the perimeter of the courtyard. Lush flowers and candles are arrayed down the center of hundreds of banquet tables. Tall potted palms waft in the breeze.

Hundreds of gold lanterns dangle overhead. The night breeze is sweet with the earthy aroma of frankincense and myrrh.

At the far end of the courtyard, dozens of uniformed musicians sit attentive with instruments resting in their laps. At each corner of the courtyard, women dressed in blue flowing robes, fervently strum tranquil melodies on graceful, gold harps.

Trumpet blasts signal Solomon and Abi's arrival. One warrior rolls a long carpet runner from the foot of the carriage to the entrance of the wedding chamber. The carriage door is opened and Solomon steps down waiving to the crowd. He reaches up to Abi and says, "Come, my darling," then assists her to the ground.

The sixty warriors hold back the antsy crowd, allowing only the wedding party and immediate family to embrace and congratulate the newlyweds. After a few moments Solomon raises his hand high above his head to still and silence the crowd. With an impish grin he reaches down, grabs the hem of his robe, and lifts it over Abi's head. His blushing bride giggles, and the mob breaks into a collective "Wooo . . ."

Solomon leans in and whispers, "I've anticipated this moment for so long. Come my darling. It's time to become one." Placing his bride's hand in the crux of his elbow, he leads her down the carpet to the wedding chamber. Bathsheba, Becca, and the wedding party in tow. Solomon opens the door, sweeps Abi off her feet and carries her inside. Outside, the witnesses get comfortable on one of the many upholstered couches on the portico.

Solomon stands in the vestibule of the wedding chamber still holding Abi in his arms. She gasps, "I can't believe this is my home. My eyes have never seen anything so beautiful. Thank you my lover!" Then lands an unexpected kiss on his lips.

“I’m so happy you are pleased.” Solomon says glowing with pride. “How about I take you on a *very* brief tour?” he says with a snicker. With his arm around her waist, Solomon guides her through their new home, ending with their luxurious bedroom suite.

“This is beyond anything I could have imagined. And our marriage bed has been set up exactly the way Ima and I designed it.” The sight of her bed relaxes her and gives her a sense of confidence as her mother’s lessons flood her mind. Pausing she inquires, “I hope you’re pleased.”

Solomon rumples his nose, “Well . . .”

Abi’s face falls. “You don’t like it?” she asks.

“It needs something . . .” he pauses, toying with her. “Us!”

“You scoundrel! You had me going.” Then, just as she had rehearsed so many times, she saunters to her bed, pulls back the silk drapery, slips inside, and signals Solomon to join her.

Lying next to his bride, Solomon’s heart begins to pound in his chest. As tempted as he is to rush things, he understands how crucial it is that Abi’s first lovemaking experience be unhurried and gratifying. Hoping to calm any possible first-time jitters, he whispers a soothing, sultry ballad:

> *You have ravished my heart*[1] *my treasure, my young wife. With one glance of your eyes and chain of your necklace my heart is pounding in my chest. You are beautiful my beloved, my treasure, my young wife. You are more intoxicating than wine, fragrant oils or spices. Your lips, my young wife, drop luscious honey from the honeycomb. Milk and honey are under your tongue.* (Song 4:9-11a)

(Evidently, French kissing was around long before France.)

---

1. Song 4:9 “Thou hast ravished my heart” (KJV) means “You have made my heart beat faster.”

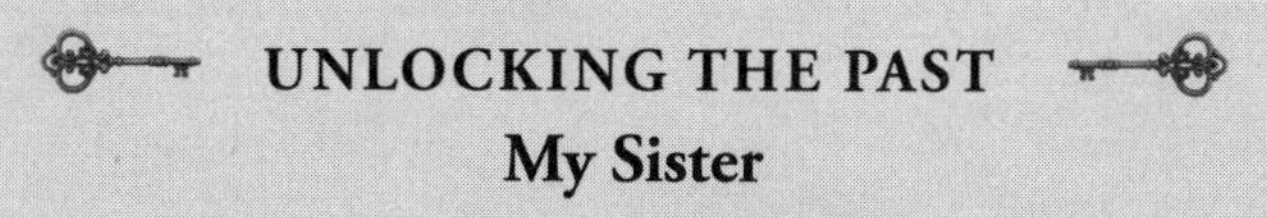

UNLOCKING THE PAST
My Sister

The Hebrew word for *sister* is *'achowth,* but it also means "beloved bride" or "treasure." The Tour Egypt website states, "One of the most affectionate titles one could call their love was 'brother' or 'sister' in ancient Egypt. This had nothing to do with sibling relations, but led many archaeologists and scholars to wrongly assume that most ancient Egyptians married their siblings."*

*Ilene Springer, "The Ancient Egyptian Bride," Tour Egypt, accessed June 19, 2020, http://www.touregypt.net/featurestories/bride.

Solomon nibbles her ear and gradually nuzzles his way down his bride's neck and shoulders, breathing her perfume in.

The fragrance of your garments is like the scent of Lebanon. You are a concealed garden,[2] *my treasure, my young wife. A spring enclosed . . . a sealed fountain . . .*[3] (Song 4:11b-12)

Solomon unfastens Abi's gown, revealing her breasts and the henna art on her waist and hips. Breathing heavily, he expresses how much her body excites him.

You are a private paradise . . .[4] *a precious reward . . .*[5] *henna [mehndi] . . . a priceless jar of nard reserved for me to open.*

2. Hebrew is *gan*: enclosed garden, a bride, or "chaste woman"
3. *spring enclosed* and *fountain sealed:* metaphors of a bride's virginity
4. *pardec:* root word paradise, an enclosed or private retreat or park
5. *meged:* precious, valuable thing

I am erect,[6] *and firm,*[7] *burning*[8] *with passion and fully aroused.*"[9] (Song 4:13-14)

UNLOCKING THE PAST
Nard

Nard, also known as spikenard, is a costly, extravagant perfume stored in small lustrous alabaster jars. The contents were so precious that the jars were sealed and preserved with wax and twine. This poetic symbolism infers that the owner had to remove the twine and break the seal before the treasured perfume inside could be enjoyed (see Mark 14:3). Another beautiful tribute to chastity.

Solomon ever so slowly kisses and caresses his way down Abi's torso to her garden. To his delight he discovers that she too is fully aroused. Comparing his virgin bride's wetness to melting snow trickling down Mount Lebanon he says, *"You are a spring*[10] *of sensual pleasure and contentment. Your excitement is like pure melting snow flowing down Mount Lebanon."* (Song 4:15)

---

6. Hebrew is *qaneh:* an erect reed, rod, shaft or bone. Also *canna*: believed to be cannabis
7. *ets:* a hard or firm object, wood, staff, bone, or man
8. *karkom:* saffron, an orange-yellow flower used to flavor drinks and induce perspiration

 qinnamown: a hot spice, cinnamon, also means erect

9. *saffron, calamus, cinnamon,* and *tree* are all analogies for heat, firmness, erection, and male excitement.
10. *ma'yan:* source of satisfaction, a spring.

UNLOCKING THE PAST
Sexual Metaphors

Notice how the metaphors in the following passage from Proverbs are in perfect alignment with the metaphors in the Song. Both use the words *drink, running water, well, springs,* and *fountain* to describe sexual pleasure. Notice that in the Song during consummation, Solomon distinguishes the Shulammite's virginity by using the words *locked, enclosed and sealed.* In the passage below, with his wife, Solomon refers to them as *private* versus *public:*

> Drink water from your own cistern,
> and running water out of your own well.
> Why should your springs flow in the streets,
> your streams of water in the public squares?
> Let them be yours alone,
> never to be shared with strangers.
> May your fountain be blessed,
> and may you rejoice in the wife of your youth:
> A loving doe, a graceful fawn—
> may her breasts satisfy you always;
> may you be captivated by her love forever. (Proverbs 5:15–19 BSB)

Burning with desire, Abi pleads with Solomon to bring her to climax. *"Awake my secret place,*[11] *come into the light.*[12] *Fan the flame*[13] *that passion may flow."*(Song 4:16a)

After reaching orgasm, she invites him to come inside. *"Come, my lover. Enter your garden, and enjoy your precious fruits."*(Song 4:16b)

The last of the sacred nuptials has been achieved. The couple is now fully *husband* and *wife.* Holding Abi in his arms, Solomon runs his

---

11. Hebrew is *tsaphown:* secret and hidden in darkness north
12. *teyman:* right, lit by the sun, south
13. *puwach:* to fan or kindle a fire, breathe

fingers through her long ringlets. "I wish I could stay right here forever. But I suppose I should get up to relieve our guests. I'm sure they're ravenous by now."

They laugh.

"I'm sure they are," Abi replies. "We probably shouldn't starve them any longer."

Reluctantly he gets up, puts on his robe, retrieves the virginity cloth from under his bride, and heads to the door to make his long-awaited announcement to the witnesses outside.

Solomon pauses, combs his tousled hair with his fingers, opens the door, clears his throat and makes his announcement, *"I have entered my garden, my treasure, my bride! I have gathered syrupy myrrh. I have eaten drippy honey from the honeycomb.*[14] *I have drunk my wine and my milk!"* (Song 5:1a) Then, as if holding a trophy, he proudly displays the damp, bloodstained virginity cloth and presents it to Becca.

The master of the banquet smiles, bows and promptly makes his way to the podium in front of the musicians. The crowd falls silent in anticipation. *"Eat, friends, and drink abundantly! Celebrate our new lovers!"* (Song 5:1b)

The royal orchestra breaks into a high-spirited tune. Young and old leap from their seats and form dance circles. The courtyard is charged with laughter and singing. Servants uncover mouthwatering buffet stations and appear from every corner carrying trays of gold goblets filled with choice wine and drink.

---

14. Hebrew is *ya'ar*: to flow or drip with honey, honeycomb
debash: syrupy, gummy, or sticky honey

Making It Relevant

Sex Celebrated!

The first time I read the customs surrounding consummation, I cringed. I thought, *Are you kidding me? I could never do that with my family and friends standing outside my door.* Talk about intimidation. I'm afraid they would have been hungry for a long, long time. But then it hit me. Back then there was no hush-hush or embarrassment associated with sex. To the contrary, it was open, honored, and celebrated—unapologetically! Not only did I find this extremely liberating, it flies in the face of just how far off track our overly conservative, prim-and-proper mindsets have taken us.

Then I had another aha moment. In the Gospels, Jesus attended a wedding in Cana, where he performed his first miracle of turning water into wine (John 2). Some scholars believe Jesus was not just a guest, they believe he officiated the ceremony. If that's so, it's very likely Jesus would have been among those standing outside the wedding chamber witnessing and blessing their union! In fact, he may have been the one who made the big announcement to the public. Wow! That gives me goosebumps. If I learned nothing else from this revelation, it shined a beautiful and liberating light on the act of marriage in a way nothing else in God's Word has ever been able to do before.

Take It Slow

I expect an entire book could be written from this one love scene. But, one thing I gleaned from it was Solomon took it slow. He didn't allow his eagerness to get the best of him. He started with praise and compliments, then kisses, then *gradually* worked his way from first base to second, then to third before waiting for the catcher to wave him in to home plate. (Didn't I tell you the men could learn something from this?)

Do you remember the '80s Motown hit by the Pointer Sisters titled "Slow Hand"? Men, if you want to make your woman swoon and beg like Shulammite did, memorize that song.

Self-Control

Remember in Song 2:7 and 3:5 when the Shulammite implored the Daughters of Jerusalem *"Do not arouse or awaken love until the time is right?"* (BSB). Solomon defines timing in Ecclesiastes 3:1, "There is a time for everything, and a season for every activity under heaven."

The season of "not yet" is over, and the season to say "yes" to her new husband has arrived. The Shulammite commands her body to wake up and let go. Have you ever noticed that self-control has a rather negative connotation to it? It's usually associated with things we're *not* supposed to do? Things we're supposed to avoid. But the other side of that coin is the ability to do what we *are* supposed to do, when we're supposed to do it. Self-control is not only the restraint to say no to the wrong person, time, or place. It's also the permission and freedom to let go and say yes to the right person, time, and place. Oh, how I wish somebody would have taught me this before my wedding night!

Orgasm

Female bodies are created with *two* pleasure points; the external clitoris and the internal G-spot. Both serve no other function than to bring sexual pleasure to a woman. This biological fact busts two myths: (1) that sex was designed strictly for procreation, and (2) that sex was created only for men to enjoy.

Male orgasm results in a flow of semen, known as *ejaculation*. Females also experience a flow during orgasm, which may or may not be noticeable depending on the intensity of the orgasm. It can take the average male as little as four minutes of stimulation to reach orgasm. But it takes the average female ten to twenty.[15]

When a man craves sex, his main objective is to reach orgasm. And men accomplish this almost 100 percent of the time through intercourse. An article on the website Our Bodies Our Selves tells us that in the 1970s a researcher "polled more than three thousand women and discovered that most of them did not experience orgasm through intercourse alone."[16] Hmmm. If men reach orgasm through intercourse, their needs are met. Conversely, if most women do not reach orgasm through intercourse, their needs are not met. Who then is actually being deprived? Not the men.

Messy Sex

On an awkward side note, many uneducated young brides are caught unaware and repulsed at the unexpected messiness of sex. In the movies and on TV you never see the women get up after intercourse to clean herself, or move away from the wet spot on the sheets after sex. It's glamorized as a clean and tidy activity. However, words like *honey, sticky*, and *drippy* aptly convey that *real-life* sex is often a damp and sweaty activity. I think comedian Bill Engvall, of the Blue Collar Comedy Tour describes it pretty succinctly . . . "hot pig sex."

---

15. Dennis Coon, *Psychology: A Modular Approach to Mind and Behavior*, 10th ed. (Belmont, CA: Thomson Wadsworth, 2006), 582.
16. OBOS Sexuality & Relationships Contributors, "Models of Sexual Response," Our Bodies Our Selves, October 15, 2011, https://www.ourbodiesourselves.org/book-excerpts/health-article/models-sexual-response/.

Oral Sex

Dr. Kevin Leman lays out his reasoning on oral sex in his formerly mentioned book *Sheet Music*. "[T]he Bible is silent on whether marital oral sex is immoral—which says to most Bible scholars that it must be okay. If God was so concerned about it, the reasoning goes, surely he would have forbidden it. Think about it—if kissing someone on the lips is okay (and I don't know of anyone who objects to this on a moral basis) why is a kiss anywhere else 'immoral'? Can a man then not kiss a woman's breasts? What about toes, or behind the knees, or other parts of the body known to be, in some people, sensitive to oral stimulation? Where do you draw the arbitrary line?"[17]

From everything I see in scripture, I don't believe the Bible is silent on oral sex. I challenge this because by now it's rather obvious that God uses poetic imagery to veil the erotic. If I'm correct, what sexual undertones do words such as *eat, consume, devour, drink, taste, spices, fruits, wine, milk, honey, sticky, drippy, sweet,* and *a goblet that never lacks blended wine* (from various Bible translations) conjure up? All of these words describe some form of eating, drinking or tasting, i.e., oral activities—which could easily symbolize oral sex.

Keeping the poetic in mind, do you still think God is silent on this topic, or simply consistently discreet?

---

17. Kevin Leman, *Sheet Music: Uncovering the Secrets of Sexual Intimacy in Marriage* (Carol Stream, IL: Tyndale House, 2010), 113.

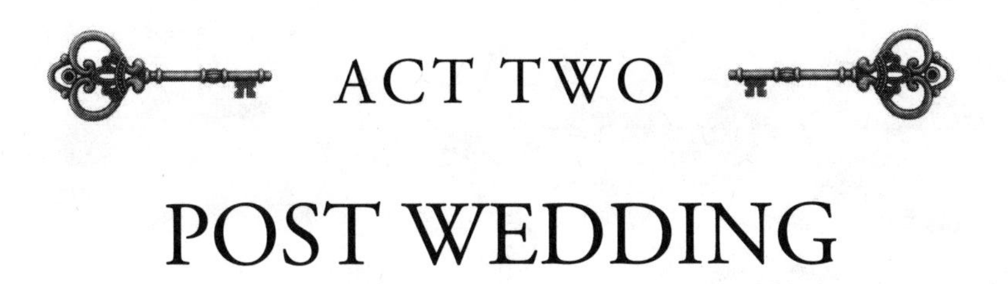

ACT TWO

POST WEDDING

CHAPTER ELEVEN

The Marriage Years Later: Betrayed and Alone

Some of you may be confused wondering, *I thought you said the Song wasn't a spiritual allegory. So far, it sounds every bit like an allegory between Christ and his church.* And, up to this point, I would agree with you. However, now that we are getting into the marriage, that theory falls apart.

The last scene of our opera ended with Solomon and his bride's consummation and the onset of their wedding banquet. So, it's my theory that Song 5:1 is the end of act 1, and Song 5:2 is the beginning of act 2—with an intermission in between. (Remember, the original Hebrew text doesn't contain punctuation, or chapter and verse numbers, to distinguish beginnings or endings.) Here's how I came to my theory:

1. Song 5:1 is a happy occasion; then suddenly, Song 5:2 is the onset of an arising conflict. It is highly doubtful this conflict took place during their honeymoon/wedding banquet.
2. *Before* the wedding, women were called "bride." *After* the wedding, they were called "wife." *Prior* to Song 5:2, Solomon

refers to the Shulammite as *ra'yah* which means "darling" or *gan* which means "virgin bride." On their wedding day he calls her *kallah* which means "young wife." *After* Song 5:2 he goes back to calling her darling, but he never refers to her as bride or young wife again.

3. Song 5:1 is almost exactly the midway point of the Song.
4. I reason that the intermission between the two acts symbolizes the passing of several years into the marriage.

I find it interesting that marriage was so important to our heavenly Father that in Deuteronomy 24:5 He instituted a law that husbands were not to leave their wives for the first year. A husband's sole purpose in life for the first 365 days and nights of marriage was to stay home and make his wife happy, happy, happy. New husbands were even exempt from being drafted to war. (In over forty years in church, I don't ever recall hearing this being preached from the pulpit.)

With this in mind, Solomon and the Shulammite's first year was likely the epitome of bliss. Can you picture it? A young couple with beautiful bodies and raging hormones, living in the lap of luxury, waking up in each other's arms, holding hands, smooching, laughing, and making spur-of-the-moment love . . . Talk about living the dream. Can it get any sweeter? Where do you go from there?

This is why it is my conjecture that Song 5:2 takes place at least seven to ten years in the future. I say this because that's usually how long it takes for time, the pressures of daily living, and complacency to set in and take their toll on even the most stable relationship.

Scripture

[The Shulammite]

I slept but my heart was awake.
Listen! My beloved is knocking:

[Solomon]

"Open to me, my sister, my darling,
my dove, my flawless one.
My head is drenched with dew,
my hair with the dampness of the night."

[The Shulammite]

I have taken off my robe—
must I put it on again?
I have washed my feet—
must I soil them again?
My beloved thrust his hand through the latch-opening;
my heart began to pound for him.
I arose to open for my beloved,
and my hands dripped with myrrh,
my fingers with flowing myrrh,
on the handles of the bolt.
I opened for my beloved,
but my beloved had left; he was gone.
My heart sank at his departure.
I looked for him but did not find him.
I called him but he did not answer.
The watchmen found me
as they made their rounds in the city.
They beat me, they bruised me;
they took away my cloak,
those watchmen of the walls!

Daughters of Jerusalem, I charge you—
if you find my beloved,
what will you tell him?
Tell him I am faint with love.

[The Daughters of Jerusalem]

How is your beloved better than others,
most beautiful of women?
How is your beloved better than others,
that you so charge us?

[The Shulammite]

My beloved is radiant and ruddy,
outstanding among ten thousand.
His head is purest gold;
his hair is wavy and black as a raven.
His eyes are like doves by the water streams,
washed in milk, mounted like jewels.
His cheeks are like beds of spice
yielding perfume.
His lips are like lilies dripping with myrrh.
His arms are rods of gold set with topaz.
His body is like polished ivory
decorated with lapis lazuli.
His legs are pillars of marble set on bases of pure gold.
His appearance is like Lebanon, choice as its cedars.
His mouth is sweetness itself; he is altogether lovely.
This is my beloved, this is my friend,
daughters of Jerusalem.

[Daughters of Jerusalem]

Where has your beloved gone,
most beautiful of women?
Which way did your beloved turn,
that we may look for him with you?

[The Shulammite]

My beloved has gone down to his garden,
to the beds of spices,
to browse in the gardens
and to gather lilies.
I am my beloved's and my beloved is mine;
he browses among the lilies.
(Song 5:2–6:3 NIV)

History and Customs

In our present-day, Western world, it's extremely hard for us to appreciate what it was like to be married three thousand years ago under Old Testament law. The old proverb, "cleanliness is next to godliness" is not scripture, but it is scripturally accurate. Make no mistake, personal hygiene is a high priority to our Heavenly Father. The entire book of Leviticus is a laundry list of rules and regulations on cleanliness and how to deal with bodily fluids, runny noses, coughs, sores, infections—and blood and semen. You see, in those days, when a woman was on her period, it was not only a messy, inconvenient nuisance, it disrupted her marriage and everybody in her household.

> *If a woman have an issue and her issue from her flesh be blood, she shall be put apart*[1] *seven days; and whosoever toucheth her shall be unclean until the evening. And every thing that she lieth upon in her separation shall be unclean; every thing also that she sitteth upon shall be unclean. And whosoever toucheth her bed shall wash his clothes and bathe himself in water, and be unclean until the evening. And whosoever toucheth any thing*

---

1. *"she shall be put apart"* in Hebrew is *niddah*: separation, set apart, menstruous, and filthy

> *that she sat upon shall wash his clothes and bathe himself in water, and be unclean until the evening. And if it be on her bed or on any thing whereon she sitteth, when he toucheth it, he shall be unclean until the evening. And if any man lie with her at all and her monthly discharge be upon him, he shall be unclean seven days; and all the bed whereon he lieth shall be unclean."* (Leviticus 15:19–24 KJ21)*

The Hebrew word *niddah* means "unclean"[2] or "set apart." Unclean persons were not permitted to enter the temple or participate in worship until they had cleansed themselves according to the Law. In fact, when a woman was on her period, she was actually called a *"niddah."*

Reflecting on the ramifications of this passage, it's easy to see how living with a *niddah* would undoubtedly contaminate the entire household and produce considerable angst. Therefore, in order to avoid unnecessary stress, *niddahs* usually moved out of the house and into the *house of uncleanness* or the *red tent* with other menstruating women.

They stayed there the five or so days of a normal period then on the seventh day (twenty-four to forty-eight hours after their period ended) the women took a full bath immediately following sunset. After this ritual cleansing, they returned home to their families (see 2 Samuel 11:4).

A Woman's Period and Sex

Let's suppose that upon waking up one morning, a couple gets involved in a little spontaneous hanky-panky, only to discover that

2. Hebrew is *tame*: religiously or ceremonially impure or unclean

the woman started her period during the night. In this situation, the couple would immediately put their passion on ice and cease activity. Both the husband and the wife would be considered unclean for seven days.

On the other hand, if a husband *knowingly* initiated sex with a woman on her period, and she consented, it was considered such a grave offense that both would be banned from atonement and cast out of the community forever.

> You shall not approach a woman to uncover her nakedness as long as she is in her customary impurity. (Leviticus 18:19 NKJV)

> If a man lies [intimately] with a woman during her menstrual cycle and uncovers her nakedness, he has exposed her flow, and she has uncovered the flow of her blood; both of them shall be cut off from their people [excluding them from the atonement made for them]. (Leviticus 20:18 AMP)

> Every garment and every leather on which there is semen shall be washed with water, and shall be unclean until evening. If a man lies with a woman so that there is a seminal emission, they shall both bathe in water and be unclean until evening. (Leviticus 15:17–18 AMP)

You see, couples were not only required to bathe after lovemaking; they were also required to launder their bedding, clothing, or any leather items that semen may have come into contact with. I don't know about you, but even with the convenience of modern-day plumbing and washing machines and dryers, this would probably make me think twice before having a spur-of-the-moment romp in the sheets. Especially in the middle of the night.

UNLOCKING THE PAST
Ancient Underwear

Leather items? You may be wondering, *Why would leather items be in their bed?"* According to Wikipedia, "the earliest and most basic garment was the '*ezor* . . . or *hagor* . . . an apron around the hips or loins, that in primitive times was made from the skins of animals. It was a simple piece of cloth worn in various modifications, but always worn next to the skin"* (see Genesis 3:21).

*Wikipedia, s.v. "biblical clothing," accessed June 20, 2020, https://en.wikipedia.org/wiki/Biblical_clothing

Harem Life in Old Testament Times

Harems were made up of wives, queens, concubines, and virgins. Esther 1 gives us keen insight into harem protocol within that region of the world during biblical times. In this chapter King Xerxes is winding up the last day of his extraordinary week-long political banquet. He and his foreign dignitaries and high-ranking officials were whooping it up and feeling no pain from the effects of the free-flowing open bar. Wanting to impress his colleagues and show off his hot trophy wife, Xerxes asked one of his eunuchs to have Queen Vashti brought to him. Vashti, who was likely dog-tired from entertaining all the high-society wives all week, snubbed his invitation.

Needless to say, Vashti's public display of disrespect for her husband in front of his peers humiliated the king. To defend his dignity and make her an example for other wives within the kingdom, Xerxes had no other recourse but to have her dethroned. She lived the rest of her days in the harem, but was never allowed to approach or see the king again.

Before we move on, it's my theory, and purely speculation, that in this segment of the Song, Solomon did to the Shulammite what Xerxes did to Vashti. In other words, when the Shulammite didn't comply with his sexual advance, he was so insulted he demoted her to his harem.

As a side note, at this point in the Shulammite's life, the Daughters of Jerusalem were likely the women she had developed relationships with, while living in the palace.

Abi's Story

Seven years have passed since the wedding, but a week ago, Abi and Solomon found themselves in the midst of misunderstanding and mayhem. Solomon got so angry he walked out on Abi and she hasn't heard from him since. Abi's cousins, Hadar and Keeva, arrived at the palace earlier in the afternoon to console and spend time with their relative.

After dinner, Abi, her cousins, and two ladies from the palace withdraw to a private balcony. It's a warm, overcast summer evening. As daylight fades, flickering wall sconces illuminate the balcony. The girls gather in close to hear their friend's account of her dreadful evening. Abi begins her sad song.

"It was about two o'clock in the morning. I was in a deep sleep. *Listen.*[3] *I heard my lover knocking. 'Open*[4] *to me my treasure, my darling, my dove, my perfect one,' he said. 'My head is damp with dew from the late-night air.'*" (Song 5:2)

---

3. Hebrew is *qowl*: voice, crying out
4. *pathach*: to open or loose oneself

UNLOCKING THE PAST
More Metaphors: Doors and Walls

Today, a sexually active, middle-aged woman might be called a "cougar." A cute, young girl might be referred to as a "fox," a "chick," or a "babe." A full-figured woman might be referred to as a "brick house." We use these modern metaphors to describe different types of women. However, during Solomon's day, women were called "doors" and "walls" (see Song 8:9). The word *door* in Hebrew is *deleth*, a metaphor for an easily accessible woman. Likewise, *wall* in Hebrew is *chowmah,* a metaphor for a chaste woman or one who is difficult to approach.

Thus, we can safely assume that a virgin was a wall. But a married woman was, or should be, a door. Therefore, it makes sense that if a wife said, "My husband is *knocking*," it didn't mean he was tapping his knuckles on a physical door asking permission to enter the room. It meant he was asking permission to enter her. He is requesting she open *herself* for sex.

This metaphor is still widely used today in many popular songs. Bruno Mars used it in "Locked Out of Heaven," and Marvin Gaye, used it in "Sexual Healing." In both of these songs men are requesting their lovers "open" for them—and we get it. Solomon is saying the exact same thing in the Song—verbatim.

In a desperate tone Abi continues her story. "I thought to myself, *My heart wanted to oblige him, but I just couldn't wake up. Half asleep I lamented, 'Honey, I disrobed and bathed my lady parts*[5] *before I went to bed. If we have sex, I'll be unclean*[6] *and have to get dressed and take another bath.' My beloved pawed*[7] *at the opening of my womb.*[8] *His desire raged for me."* (Song 5:2-4a)

---

5. Hebrew is *regel*: a euphemism for *pudenda* or female genitals
6. *tanaph*: to defile, dirty or soil
7. *yad*: hand, phallos, penis, member of body
8. *chowr: hole, cavity, socket, latch*/*me'ah:* bowels, womb

"Awww . . . You poor girl . . ." Hadar sympathizes. "You must have been completely out of it."

Still weeping, Abi replies, "I was. I was so groggy . . . To tell you the truth I'm not really sure what happened. I think I drifted back to sleep for a few minutes. Because the next thing I remember thinking was, *I'll wake up and open for my lover. I dipped my hand in myrrh . . . With fingers dripping with myrrh I passed them over the hollow of my thigh*[9] *to unlock*[10] *myself for my lover. Then I called out to him . . . but my heart sank when I realized he was gone.*"(Song 5:4b-6a)

"Did you get up and look for him? Did you find him?" Keeva inquires.

"Yes, I got up," Abi nodded. "I put on my cloak and veil and *searched for him but didn't find him. I called for him but he didn't answer. I ran into the keeper of the women walking the palace halls.* Solomon must have told him what happened. *He chastised and ridiculed me. Then the keeper of the women grabbed my veil and ripped it off my head!*"(Song 5:6b-7)

UNLOCKING THE PAST
Women's Head Coverings

The Hebrew word for *cloak* is *radiyd,* a feminine scarf that covered the head, but not the face. During the Mesopotamian (Assyrian) Era and the Persian Empire (1400–600 BC), it was customary for women to wear scarves and shawls in various configurations to indicate different levels of status and aristocratic rank.

Women with loose moral standards were publicly exposed and shamed by having their coverings removed or the heads shorn. If a woman intentionally appeared in public with her head uncovered, it was considered an act of rebellion against her husband and grounds for divorce (see 1 Corinthians 11:5–6 *NIV Study Bible* footnote).

9. Hebrew is *kaph:* hollow of thigh joint

10. *man'uwl:* socket of hip, thigh, lock, bolt

Now sobbing and barely intelligible, Abi goes on. "I tried to cover my naked head with my arms. I ran back to my room and cried till the sun came up."

"That's awful," Hadar says, getting up and wrapping her arms around her friend. "No wonder you're a wreck."

Hanging her head Abi continues, "How could this happen? We had something so special. Now it's a living nightmare. It's been over a week since he left . . . every day that passes makes me wonder if he's ever coming back."

In an attempt to calm her, one of the ladies replies, "Oh, darling, I'm so, so sorry. Surely he'll cool off . . . I'm sure he'll come to his senses . . . He'll come back."

Hoping they might see Solomon, Abi begs them to relay a message. *"Daughters of Jerusalem, if you see my beloved, promise me you will tell him that I am sick with grief and love."*(Song 5:8)

The other girl doesn't understand how she could possibly want him back. She probes, *"Most Beautiful of Women, what's so special about Solomon over other men that you would ask us to do such a thing?* You deserve better." (Song 5:9)

Abi closes her eyes and answers in a soft lullaby.

> *My lover is the light of my life. He is handsome and distinguished above ten thousand men. He is a leader—refined like pure gold. His hair is thick and wavy, black as a raven. His eyes are doves bathing in streams of milk. Being married to him is a delight. His cheeks are soft and smell of sweet spice. His lips are music, dripping wisdom and inspiration, more priceless than myrrh. His hands are strong, with gold rings and precious gems. His chest is chiseled ivory, inlaid with sapphire veins. His legs are alabaster pillars set in sockets of pure gold. His presence is as splendid as the cedars of Lebanon. His lips are sweet and*

utterly desirable. He is my lover. He is my friend, O Daughters of Jerusalem. (Song 5:10-16)

Wanting desperately to ease their friend's pain, the girls go along with her request. *"Most Beautiful of Women, where did your lover disappear? Where did he go? Tell us. We'll help you find him."* (Song 6:1)

Abi knows exactly where he has gone. She composes herself, stares into space and numbly states: *"My lover has gone to his harem in the southern region . . . To his brides, beds of passion and virgins. I belonged to him and he belonged to me . . . But now he spends his time among the virgins."*(Song 6:2-3)

She breaks down again. The ladies huddle around and stroke her hair. There simply are no words suitable to comfort her.

Making It Relevant

Complacency

All marriages wax and wane. Sooner or later all couples fall prey to some form of complacency. It's inevitable. Solomon and the Shulammite's marriage began with a fairy-tale honeymoon. Their first night together, Solomon approached his bride with loving compliments, kisses, and caresses and made slow, unselfish love to her. In contrast, seven or so years later, he wanders home in the middle of the night, throws a few meaningless compliments at his sleeping wife, and gropes her. No kisses, no caresses, no embrace . . .

On the other hand, maybe I'm completely off base. Maybe it was the Shulammite who had grown complacent. Maybe her beautiful song of praise about Solomon indicates a reawakening to what she'd had all along—but had taken for granted. I've witnessed countless wives and husbands whose favorite pastime was complaining about their spouses—until the day they walked out. Then, miraculously, they discovered a newfound appreciation for what they'd had all along. Perhaps both of them had become complacent.

Sex on Demand

For decades, every interpretation I studied on this scene shamed the Shulammite for depriving her husband's *need* for sex. They based their conclusion on the following passage:

> The husband should fulfill his marital duty to his wife, and likewise the wife to her husband. The wife's body does not belong to her alone but also to her husband. In the same way, the husband's body does not belong to him alone but also to his wife. Do not deprive each other except my mutual consent for a time, so that you may devote yourselves to prayer. Then come together again so that Satan will not tempt you because of your lack of self control. I say this as a concession, not as a command. (1 Corinthians 7:3-6)

Am I the first person to challenge this judgment? First, let me preface this by saying *all* the interpretations I'm referring to were written by men, and second, the *command* they claimed she broke hadn't even been written yet—not for another thousand years. Oh, and did you catch the last line of this passage? The line that is often omitted? "I say this as a concession, *not a command?"* Oops. In my opinion, this do-not-deprive, sex-on-demand tactic taught for so many years, may have won men the battle, but it's ultimately losing them the war.

As a woman, I perceive this scene in the Song from a completely different angle. I see an exhausted woman, in a dead sleep, with a husband, who prances in, in the wee hours of the morning with a dire case of the hots, wakes her up and wants sex—now. I thought to myself, *Since when is his* ***need*** *for sex more important than her* ***need*** *for sleep.*

God is love. He is patient, kind, and doesn't demand His way (see 1 Corinthians 13). He loves a cheerful giver (see 2 Corinthians 9:7). Don't we understand that whenever we deny someone of their freedom to give, it only breeds resentment and bitterness—not love and intimacy? Why in all other areas of life do we teach that its good and right to maintain healthy boundaries, and to say "no" when appropriate, but for some ridiculous reason, in the closest and most intimate of all relationships, that doesn't apply?

For centuries our enemy has done an incredibly underhanded job of robbing women of their God-given rights. We've been led to believe that women's needs, feelings, bodies, salaries, votes, and gifts are less important than men's. Please understand me. I'm not saying husbands are not the head of the family. Nor am I denying that God has given them authority to have the final say in disputable matters. However, that same authority should be implemented with a love so deep, that it's also prepared to die for their wives if need be. In that context, a little death might take the form of a cold shower on occasion.

Masturbation

You're probably wondering, *Kim, did I understand Abi's story correctly? Are you suggesting that in Song 5:5, when the Shulammite dipped her hands in oil of myrrh and stroked herself between her thighs, that she was masturbating?* It would seem so. That's why I provided so many Hebrew definitions in the footnotes. So you can read them and decide for yourself.

Let's be frank, lubrication is ***essential*** for intercourse. It is literally the ***key*** that unlocks a woman for penetration. Subsequently, the only way the Shulammite could physically accommodate Solomon's demand for a midnight quickie, was to speed up the process by lubricating and stimulating herself with oil of myrrh.

Which likely leads you to another question. *Kim, if you're correct, does it mean masturbation is allowed?* Yes and no. It depends. Masturbation is a complex and highly controversial topic and should be weighed with extreme caution and in alignment with scripture. Why is it complex? Because what makes it right or wrong is not the act itself; it's the *reason* or the *why* the act is being done.

Many claim the Bible is silent on masturbation. After discovering this passage I respectfully disagree. I do however, believe Jesus publicly condemned masturbation while looking at or thinking about someone other than your spouse. In his famous Sermon on the Mount, in front of thousands of men and women, Jesus made the following audacious statement:

> You have heard that it was said, 'You shall not commit adultery.' But I tell you that anyone who looks at a woman lustfully has already committed adultery with her in his heart. If your right eye causes you to stumble, gouge it out and throw it away. It is better for you to lose one part of your body than for your whole body to be thrown into hell. *And if your right hand causes you to stumble, cut it off and throw it away* (emphasis added). It is better for you to lose one part of your body than for your whole body to go into hell. (Matthew 5:27–30)

Can you imagine the awkwardness and giggles that fell over the crowd when He said that?! Make no mistake—all four verses of this segment have to do with lust. Jesus didn't all of a sudden switch from adultery to stealing mid-stream. And every adult in the crowd (wink, wink) knew exactly what He was getting at.

On the other side of the spectrum, if a marriage is going through a challenging season, such as a long-term illness, injury, or a deployment, then by all means, use masturbation to fill the gap. If it's needed to prime yourself or your partner for sex the way the Shulammite did, use it. In the aforementioned book *A Celebration of Sex,* Dr. Douglas Rosenau explains one of the benefits of masturbation, "Because of the excessive baggage the word *masturbation* carries with it, it is preferable to use the descriptive words *genital pleasuring* in the context of making love. . . I think, especially as a wife is working to become more easily orgasmic, personal pleasuring can be a gift to the marriage in self-discovery. . . If we aren't careful, we can become legalistic in never touching ourselves. . . Work beyond the fear of self-stimulation or being selfish and learn to play together."[11]

If you're still confused, the Apostle Paul gave us a litmus test for anything and everything, including masturbation.

> "Everything is permissible"—but not everything is beneficial.
> "Everything is permissible"—but not everything is constructive.
> Nobody should seek his own good, but the good of others.
> (1 Corinthians 10:23–24)

> "Everything is permissible for me,"—but not everything is beneficial.
> "Everything is permissible for me"—but I will not be mastered by anything. (1 Corinthians 6:12 BSB)

At first glance, these passages appear almost identical. However, the first seeks the benefit of the relationship. The second defines an addiction or something that controls us. In light of these passages, ask yourself, *Are we using masturbation to enhance or improve our lovemaking and relationship?* Or, *am using it to gratify myself in place of my spouse? Does it control me? Can I stop? Am I addicted?*

---

11. Douglas E. Rosenau, *A Celebration of Sex: A Guide to Enjoying God's Gift of Sexual Intimacy* (Nashville, TN: Thomas Nelson, 2001), 131, 132.

CHAPTER TWELVE

A Confrontational Reunion: "Can I Forgive Him?"

When Solomon and the Shulammite's mother sat down before the betrothal banquet to negotiate her daughter's *ketubah,* there is no way we can possibly know the terms they agreed to. However, I think it's reasonable to assume that the Shulammite and her mother both anticipated that Solomon would probably take a few wives for political reasons. After all, that's just what kings did. But, I think it's highly unlikely that the Shulammite or her mother, or any wife in her right mind for that matter, would have agreed to share her husband with 999 other women!

It's my position that when Solomon walked out on the Shulammite, he stayed gone for months—possibly years. And while he was away, he inducted an outrageous amount of queens and concubines into his harem—sixty queens and eighty concubines to be exact (Song 6:8). I contend that after the thrill of new women subsided, he began to miss the intimacy and relationship he had with his best friend and lover and wanted her back. The following segment is the awkward and painful reunion between him and the Shulammite.

Scripture

[Solomon]

You are as beautiful, my darling, as Tirzah,
as lovely as Jerusalem,
as majestic as troops with banners.
Turn your eyes away from me,
for they have overcome me.
Your hair is like a flock of goats
streaming down from Gilead.
Your teeth are like a flock of sheep
coming up from the washing;
each has its twin,
and not one of them is lost.
Your brow behind your veil
is like a slice of pomegranate.
There are sixty queens and eighty concubines,
and maidens without number,
but my dove, my perfect one, is unique,

[The Daughters of Jerusalem]

the favorite of the mother who bore her.
The maidens see her and call her blessed;
the queens and concubines sing her praises.

Who is this who shines like the dawn,
as fair as the moon,
as bright as the sun,
as majestic as the stars in procession?

[The Shulammite]

I went down to the walnut grove
to see the blossoms of the valley,
to see if the vines were budding
or the pomegranates were in bloom.
Before I realized it, my desire had set me
among the royal chariots of my people.

[The Messengers]

Come back, come back, O Shulammite!
Come back, come back, that we may gaze upon you.
(Song 6:4–13a BSB)

History and Customs

In Genesis 2:22–24, God defines his intent for monogamous marriage as the union of one man and one woman, becoming "one flesh." Experts agree God did not approve of polygamous marriages, but He did *allow* them. It doesn't take a scholar to realize that virtually every polygamous marriage recorded in the Bible was riddled with jealousy and drama. The households of David, Jacob, Abraham and Moses, to name just a few, were rift with rivalry and contention. Because unfair favoritism had become such a problem in polygamous marriages, God mercifully provided a way out for wives who found themselves in an abusive and loveless marriage: "If her master marries another wife, he may not reduce her food, her clothing, or her privilege [conjugal rights] as a wife. If he does not do these three things for her, then shall she leave free, without *payment of* money" (Exodus 21:10–11 AMP).

Most resources believe David had eight wives and at least ten concubines (see 2 Samuel 15:16). In stark contrast, Solomon had seven hundred wives and three hundred concubines. Exactly one thousand women. That's an insane amount of bed partners. Recognizing how driven and over-the-top Solomon was, I can't help but wonder if one of his goals in life was to be hailed as the first (maybe only) king to own a harem of exactly one thousand women.

Wives

First Kings 11:3 tells us that Solomon's seven hundred wives were of "royal birth." The word "royal" implies that all seven hundred were used to seal political treaties and alliances with kings from foreign countries. Solomon took these wives in spite of the fact that God warned Israelites not to intermarry with foreigners (Deuteronomy 7:1–4; 17:17). Chances are he justified his actions as strictly *business.* But, eventually he did exactly what God knew any of us would do when we team ourselves with unbelievers (see 2 Corinthians 6:14). He succumbed to their beauty and charm, then caved to their unbiblical ideologies and man-made gods.

Concubines

Concubines were much like mistresses of today. Upon sleeping with a man, they became his property and were considered a lower status than a wife. They didn't have a *ketubah,* bride price, wedding ceremony, or divorce rights to protect them. Most resources agree that concubines were obtained strictly for sex and childbearing. It stands to reason that only kings or very wealthy men could financially provide for the needs of multiple wives, concubines, and their subsequent offspring.

Eunuchs

Eunuchs were males who were born either impotent, with a genital defect, or castrated for the specific purpose of working in a royal harem. According to *Gesenius' Hebrew-Chaldee Lexicon*, normal, young boys were involuntarily recruited and made into eunuchs by soaking their testicles in hot water and then crushing or mutilating them until they dissolved (see Deuteronomy 23:1). Eunuchs were considered a lower social status than the average male servant.

Here's something to ponder. Do you think that maybe, Joseph's wrongful imprisonment, stemming from the false sexual accusations brought against him by Potiphar's wife, is why only eunuchs were permitted to work in royal harems (see Genesis 39)?

Abi's Story

It's been almost two years since Solomon walked out on Abi. She has made peace with her new life and now lives in a charming harem suite. Lounging in her robe, enjoying the warmth of the morning sunshine at a small table by the window, she gulps down her last bite of pineapple and cheese curds. Interrupted by a faint knock at the door, she opens the door slightly and peeks through the opening. She bats her eyes in bewilderment at the keeper of the women who ripped her scarf from her head on that dreadful night so long ago.

He shoves a note in her face and blurts, "This is for you," then hurries down the hall.

Solomon's royal blue seal is stamped on the note. Her hands tremble as she breaks the seal and unfolds the paper. She slumps on to a nearby couch. It reads:

My Beloved,
I have returned to Jerusalem. I long to see you. Please meet me this evening in our wedding chamber.
Solomon

Month after month she pleaded with God for this moment. But now she wants nothing to do with him. Impulsively she runs down the hall bare-footed and taps on her friend Libi's door. Impatient for an answer, she barges in.

"My goodness! You're up bright and early," Libi chirps.

Glum-faced, Abi hands her the note, plops herself down on the bed, and waits for her response.

Libi reads the note slowly, then appears to read it again, silently mouthing the words as she reads the second time. Finally, she looks up at her friend and with an anguished expression says, "Do you want to see him?"

"No, I don't," Abi says adamantly. "What do you think he wants? Do you think he expects me to sleep with him?"

"You won't know unless you go," Libi responds, shaking her head. "You really have no choice but to go . . . and see what this is all about."

"I'm confused," Abi says, rubbing her forehead as if in pain. "Why now . . . after all this time?"

"I wish I could answer that. But you're the strongest women I've ever known, and you are going to get through this," her friend reassures her. "I tell you what. You go get a bath. I'll get a couple of the other girls, and we'll be waiting for you in your suite when you get back. We'll spend the day with you and help you get ready. How does that sound?"

"I guess," Abi sighs pitifully. "What options do I have? You're such a great friend. I don't know what I'd do without you." She hugs Libi, turns and walks down the hall, then whimpers over her shoulder, "I'll be back in about an hour."

When Abi returns to her room, three friends are waiting for her as promised. Each one gives her a warm hug. Libi says, "Look. While you were bathing, we took the liberty of putting together a few outfits for you to choose from. Jewelry, shoes . . . the whole ensemble." She points to the clothes lying on the bed. "What do you think?"

"I think you ladies are amazing. That's what I think," Abi replies. "The last thing I want to worry about is what to wear tonight."

The girls work hard at keeping the mood upbeat and encouraging as she gets ready. One girl quips, "One look at you and he's going to realize what an idiot he was for leaving you!" Then, realizing she was talking about the king, she quickly adds, "Oh my! Please don't repeat that or he'll have me demoted to chambermaid."

Everyone chuckles.

"Don't worry. He knows he was an idiot. That's why he's back," Libi snorts. "Now girls, it's getting late. What do you say we give Abi a little time to herself before she leaves?"

Each girl hugs and encourages their friend before they walk out the door. "You're a strong, confident woman," says one.

"You're going to do just fine," says another.

"We'll be waiting in the courtyard when you get back," Libi says, blowing her a kiss and closing the door behind her.

Abi finishes getting dressed, then sits a few moments in subdued prayer before making her slow, reluctant walk across the palace grounds to the wedding chamber.

Solomon, eager to see his beloved, arrives early and wanders the still, familiar halls of their wedding chamber. He sinks into his favorite chair in the parlor and lets out a long sigh, anxious to see Abi's smiling face.

Stepping onto the portico, Abi takes a firm grip of the large lever on the copper-embossed chamber door. She pauses, takes a deep breath, then slowly pushes the door open. As she steps into the vestibule, the pain of their last evening there comes crashing back like a violent flood. Suddenly and very unexpectedly, anger rises up inside her. *How dare he just abandon me like that? And for so long? He never even gave me a chance to explain. I don't deserve to be treated like this.*

With righteous indignation simmering inside her, she pulls her shoulders back and juts her chin forward. With a restrained huff she enters the parlor. Solomon, still as handsome as the day he left, smiles and stands to greet her. She confronts him face-to-face, her piercing eyes fixed on his.

Abi's glare throws Solomon off guard. He stammers for words to break the hostile silence. Using old familiar lines, he sings, *"You are beautiful, my darling, as delightful as Tirzah,*[1] *as lovely as Jerusalem. But you are as dreadful as an advancing army.*[2] *Turn your eyes away from me, for they rage against me."*[3] (Song 6:4-5)

Unmoved, she maintains her stance, solemn and silent.

Fumbling for words, he describes her as he did on their wedding day, "You are just as beautiful as the day we wed. *Your tresses are like shiny, ebony goats descending Mount Gilead. Your smile is as brilliant as ewes after their washing. Not one is missing. Your cheeks behind your veil are like the blush of a pomegranate."* (Song 6:6-7)

---

1. *Tirzah:* my delight
2. Hebrew is *'ayom*: frightful, terrible, and formidable
   dagal: conspicuous, host of soldiers, raise a flag, troop with banners
3. *rahab:* to rage or storm against

UNLOCKING THE PAST
Solomon's Age

In Song 5:11, the Shulammite described Solomon's hair as thick and black as a raven, giving us a sound clue that he was still young at this stage of the story. In addition, Solomon's confession of *sixty* queens and *eighty* concubines (Song 6:8) is further evidence that this scene took place during the younger and earlier years of his reign.

Solomon recalling their wedding day only incites her anger. He realizes his attempt at small talk is only making matters worse. Clearly, she has no intentions of letting him stroll back into her life and pretend as if nothing happened. Anything short of admitting the truth is futile. After another long, uncomfortable pause, he confesses, *"Yes, I've been in my harem. I have sixty queens, eighty concubines, and more virgins than I can count. But my dove, you're still my favorite. There is no one like you."* (Song 6:8-9a)

UNLOCKING THE PAST
Sixty Queens, Eighty Concubines

Let's camp on the sixty queens and eighty concubines for a moment and do a bit of math. If Solomon married a different queen every week for sixty consecutive weeks, it would have taken fourteen months. If he slept with a different concubine every night for eighty nights in a row, it would have taken two and a half months.

If we add the two together, it would have taken him a minimum of a year and a half to induct that many women into his harem. Is it plausible to suppose that when Solomon went down to his southern harem, he found himself caught up in a sex binge that went on for many months, maybe even years?

Favorite? Favorite? The thought makes her blood boil. *We were best friends, husband and wife—not casual sex partners. We shared our hopes, dreams, and fears with each other.* The idea of being his number-one, go-to girl is not something she's willing to settle for. To her own shock, she does an about-face and marches out of the chamber, leaving the king dumbfounded.

Her walk back to the harem is a blur. Entering the courtyard, her friends are sitting around a marble fountain just like they promised. "That was fast." Libi calls out. "We didn't expect you back so soon."

As Abi gets closer, Libi's eyes widen, "Oh my! You look like a woman on the warpath."

Abi storms past them, babbling under her breath.

Chasing her to her room, the girls hurl questions at her, "What happened?" "What did he say?" "Was he mean to you?"

"I knew it was a bad idea to see him again," she fumes. "Not only has he been with his harem all this time; he has sixty new queens and eighty concubines! Yes. You heard right. Sixty queens and eighty concubines! Did he really think I would welcome him back with open arms like nothing happened? I could never be with him again." She throws a small bag on the bed and tosses clothing and personal items into it.

"What are you doing?" Libi asks in horror.

"I don't know. I just know . . . I need to think. I need to get away from here."

"But where will you go?" they ask.

Shaking her head, half-crying, half-ranting, she states, "I have no idea. I'm not sure of anything right now."

She wraps her cloak around her shoulders and hugs and kisses her friends on the cheek. Then she storms out the door, and without another word flees the palace.

The Daughters stand in the doorway and wave as they watch the woman they respect and admire courageously walk away from the palace. *"She was her mother's only daughter and favorite child. Sweet and kind. The virgins look up to her. The queens and concubines sing her praises. Who is this angel from heaven that appears like the dawn; as beautiful as the moon, as pure as the sun, as dreadful as the stars in procession?"*[4] (Song 6:9b-10)

Distraught and confused, Abi seeks solace at the inn in the valley. It's a small inn nestled in a grove of walnut trees—quiet and peaceful. After dropping her bag in her room, she takes a walk through the Persian nut grove and leans against one of the tall trees. Her tension and anger melt into sadness, and she weeps in the privacy of the orchard. *How do I move forward from here?* she wonders. *How can I possibly be with him again and ever feel the same?* Seeing him again brought back feelings she thought were dead. But all she can envision is his body intertwined with all those women. The images bring a surge of tears.

Looking into the moonlit sky, she sings with a whisper, *"I came to the valley of Persian nut trees to see if there was a spark of love left in me, after the hell I've endured. To see if there was any passion left to salvage. Deep in my soul,[5] I knew I'd have to go back to the chariots of my people."* (Song 6:11-12)

After what feels like hours and an ocean of tears, she returns to her room and collapses into bed, exhausted.

The next morning Abi wakes late, her head throbbing and her body numb. Oblivious to her grey mood, the sun shines brightly through the window of her room. *Maybe getting outside will help*, she muses. After a few bites of fruit and bread for breakfast, she wanders into the valley and finds a stream. The sun has warmed a large rock beside the water, so she sits down and closes her eyes, listening intently to the sound of the trickling brook. If only the water could wash the past away and take

4. Hebrew is *ayom dagal,* the same words used in Song 6:4, however they are translated differently.

5. *yada'*: to be revealed

them back to the couple they were before all the hurt and pain. Back to the couple who had it all . . .

Two months have passed, and Abi is still at the inn. Solomon can't get the anguish and betrayal he saw in her eyes out of his mind. Gad invites Solomon to go for a horseback ride through the countryside. Wandering through the huge cedars, Solomon confides in his friend, "Gad, You know how much I adored Abi. I don't know what came over me that night. I was so, so angry . . . My anger blinded me. When I left I never dreamed I'd stay away more than a few days. But when I got to the southern harem, the women were all over me . . . They flattered me. I was drunk on it. Until now I never let myself think about what it must have done to Abi. I betrayed her . . ."

"It's obvious you still love her very much," Gad replies. "We've been friends since we were boys. Are you asking for my advice?

"Yes. Yes . . . Be honest with me," he begs.

Gad pauses, mustering up the words and the courage to say what Solomon needs to hear. "Do you love her enough to give up the harem? To be accountable?"

"I do love her. I really do . . ." Solomon says, hanging his head. "But it's going to be hard . . . really hard."

"Yes, it will." Gad nods. "It's ultimately your resolve that will make it work. But I'm here for you if you need me. You are a powerful and disciplined man. I know you are capable of doing whatever you set your mind to."

After returning to the palace, Solomon sits at his desk and reflects on their conversation. *I want her back, but not because I'm king, or because she is forced to come back—but because she wants to.* He writes her a short note and instructs his messengers to find her and deliver it to her.

After lunch, Abi goes back to her favorite rock by the stream to pray. Sitting in the warm sunlight, she leans against a tree, closes her eyes, and listens to the sound of the water. She knows she can't stay at the inn forever—sooner or later she has to go back. The problem is she never stopped loving Solomon. Nevertheless, she would rather continue to live in the harem, the way she was, than compete with all the other women in Solomon's life.

"Your highness. Your highness."

Abi wakes up, unaware she dozed off. *Am I dreaming? Am I hearing things?* she wonders. *I haven't been called your highness in years.* Two of the king's messengers stand nearby.

"We have a message from King Solomon for you," says one of the men. He pulls out a note stamped with the royal seal and reads, *"Come back, Mrs. Solomon. Come back, Solomon's girl. Return so we can restore the love we once knew."*[6] (Song 6:13a)

He hadn't called her by that nickname since the early years of their marriage. Calling her "Mrs. Solomon" and "Solomon's girl" communicates loud and clear that he wants her back as his wife and one-and-only. Those words gave her the hope and strength she needed for healing to begin.

Without delay she gathers her belongings at the inn and returns to the palace with the messengers. Upon arrival, the keeper of the women greets her with an awkward but warm welcome. As she follows him, she expects to be led to the harem, but instead he leads her to their wedding chamber. To her astonishment, all her belongings have been returned and put away in their rightful place.

---

6. Hebrew is *showb*: to return and restore
Shulammite: pet name meaning "Mrs. Solomon" or "Solomon's girl."

"Is everything the way you like it?" the keeper asks.

"Why . . . Yes. It's, it's . . . perfect." she replies bewildered.

"Very well. If you need anything, I'll be back to check on you in the morning." He pauses, hands her another sealed note from Solomon, then closes the door and bids her good night. She opens the note. It reads:

> *Welcome home Shulammite,*
> *Take all the time you need. I'll join you when you are ready.*
>
> *Your beloved,*
> *Solomon.*

Abi's heart stings. She thinks to herself, *Starting over is going to be a long painful process. But, if there's a chance we can restore the love we once had, I'm willing to risk it all.*

Making It Relevant

Sex Addiction

I don't think anybody would argue that a thousand-woman harem is an obscene amount of women. Even if Solomon could somehow justify that many political wives, how could he justify three hundred concubines? Surely he didn't need more children. Yet, in all my years, I've never heard anyone suggest that Solomon had a sex addiction. Think about it, Hugh Hefner possessed a meager fifty women in his infamous *Playboy* harem, yet nobody had an issue labeling him a sex addict.

I was apprehensive about making such a bold statement against the wisest man to ever live, until I came across another condemning clue. Back in Song 5:2 Solomon traipsed in, in the middle of the night, looking for sex, and the Shulammite described it as, "*My lover is knocking*"

(EHV). This particular Hebrew word for *knock* is *daphaq* and it not only means "to knock," it means "to beat, press severely," or "to overdrive a flock." This harsh word implies he wasn't just asking, he was demanding, and demanding often. This word leads me to believe he had such an insatiable appetite that the Shulammite simply could not keep up with him.

Men today don't have physical harems, they have virtual harems. They are seduced into online porn. As a result, husbands often try to get their wives to recreate these fantasies for them in real life. Don't get me wrong, I'm all for being playful and creative in the bedroom, but real wives will never be able to live up to the photoshopped and hyped illusions portrayed on the screen. It will likely start out as fun and adventurous, but one of the many problems with porn is it leads down a slippery-slope and top-that mindset. As with all addictions, enough will *never* be enough. Sooner or later performance will take over and intimacy will be smothered out.

Unfaithfulness

When we get married we make a lifelong oath before God and witnesses to *forsake all others and to meet our husband or wife's consortium needs.* Changing our minds on either of these two promises five, ten, or twenty years down the road, is not an option. Because sexual intimacy is what sets marriage apart from all other relationships, I'm convinced that there is more than one way to be unfaithful. The first is the sin of adultery, the sin of commission (Matthew 5:32). But I also believe cheating your spouse out of their conjugal rights, the sin of omission, is also unfaithfulness (James 4:17).

How can I justify making such a daring statement? Remember at the beginning of the chapter we learned that during Old Testament times, wives were not allowed to divorce their husbands *for any reason*. Yet in Exodus 21:10-11, God gave wives permission to leave their husbands without penalty if her husband did not provide basic necessities such as food, clothing, or sex. Maybe I'm missing something, but if a wife could leave her husband because he denied her conjugal rights under the Law, then why wouldn't that reasoning also hold true today for either spouse under grace?

CHAPTER THIRTEEN

Healing, Reconciliation, and Renewal

Let me warn you: this chapter will frustrate the old-school Baptists and traditionalists. Why? Because in this scene, the Shulammite is doing the unmentionable: she is dancing . . . nude! Wearing nothing more than a few pieces of jewelry, a sash made of lilies, and strappy, little sandals. It's known as the dance of *Mahanaim*. Now watch how the cultural and historical discoveries surrounding this playful tradition bring this dynamic love scene to life.

Scripture

[The Shulammite]

Why do you look at the Shulammite,
as on the dance of Mahanaim?

[Solomon]

How beautiful are your sandaled feet,
O daughter of the prince!
The curves of your thighs are like jewels,
the handiwork of a master.
Your navel is a rounded goblet;
it never lacks blended wine.
Your waist is a mound of wheat
encircled by the lilies.
Your breasts are like two fawns,
twins of a gazelle.
Your neck is like a tower
made of ivory;
your eyes are like the pools of Heshbon
by the gate of Bath-rabbim;
your nose is like the tower of Lebanon,
facing toward Damascus.
Your head crowns you like Mount Carmel,
the hair of your head like purple threads;
the king is captured in your tresses.

How fair and pleasant you are,
O love, with your delights!
Your stature is like a palm tree;
your breasts are clusters of fruit.
I said, "I will climb the palm tree;
I will take hold of its fruit."
May your breasts be like clusters of the vine,
the fragrance of your breath like apples,
and your mouth like the finest wine.

[The Shulammite]

May it flow smoothly to my beloved,
gliding gently over lips and teeth.
I belong to my beloved,
and his desire is for me.
Come, my beloved,
let us go to the countryside;
let us spend the night among the wildflowers.
Let us go early to the vineyards
to see if the vine has budded,
if the blossom has opened,
if the pomegranates are in bloom—
there I will give you my love.
The mandrakes send forth a fragrance,
and at our door is every delicacy,
new as well as old,
that I have treasured up for you, my beloved.
(Song 6:13b-7:13 BSB)

History and Customs

Today, we hold entertainment in the palm of our hand. With the swipe of a finger, we can listen to music, watch a movie, play a game, or read a novel. Now try imagining what life was like without internet, cell phones, television or even electricity. We'd have no choice but to gather beside the light of a fire and entertain each other playing cards, board games, telling tales, strumming a guitar, singing, and yes . . . dancing.

Did you know that during Old Testament times women were quite the instrumentalists? It's true. One of the popular pastimes of the day was women playing flutes, harps, and tambourines while dancing in circles. Tambourines were also called hand drums, timbrels, or frame drums (see Psalms 68:25). In Exodus 15 Miriam, accompanied by many other ladies, sang, danced, and played hand drums after Israel's illustrious march through the Red Sea. We see it again after an unknown teenage shepherd, named David, took down the offensive Philistine giant Goliath, with nothing more than a slingshot and a stone. To celebrate this extraordinary victory, young girls from surrounding towns gathered in the streets of Jerusalem to play hand drums, sing and dance (1 Samuel 18:6).

Hand Drums

In an article titled "Women with Hand-Drums," the author states, "Archaeological evidence suggests in virtually every instance, the frame-drum players are female . . . This evidence, along with cross-cultural materials suggests . . . that the playing of these percussion instruments was a specifically female role in the ancient Mediterranean world."[1]

Ancient hieroglyphics of dancing women playing frame drums, flutes, and lyres are engraved on countless walls of Egyptian pyramids and ruins. Another fascinating discovery is that in many of these historical etchings, the women are dancing in the buff, wearing only see-through clothing, jewelry and/or a sash around their waists or hips.

Dance

Have you ever noticed that most women are born with a dance gene? They instinctively love to dance. And men instinctively love to watch!

---

1. Carol Meyers, "Women with Hand-Drums, Dancing: Bible," *The Encyclopedia of Jewish Women*, Jewish Women's Archive, accessed June 26, 2020, https://jwa.org/encyclopedia/article/women-with-hand-drums-dancing-bible.

If you don't believe me, next time you're at a wedding reception, watch what happens on the dance floor as the night progresses. Women let their hair down, kick off their shoes and take over the dance floor, while men stand on the sidelines and watch.

Dancing is fun, and it's good for you. It's great cardio, it tones the body, and it improves flexibility. It also has psychological benefits—especially for women. When women allow themselves to get lost in the music and rhythm of a sensual beat, swaying their hips and shimmying their breasts, it makes them feel alive and sexy. ***Erotic dance not only turns men into goo; it revs up the female libido.*** In Dr. Rosenau's previously mentioned book, *A Celebration of Sex,* he states, "Your feminine power actually arouses you sexually and plays a part in your assertive sexual desire. This is called alluring desire and is a fun aspect of who you are as a woman . . . Actively seducing your husband by playing on his visual nature so he grins all day and you delight in your femininity, or fun flirting and teasing that increase the playfulness and fun in your sexual companionship are examples of a definite win-win and worth cultivating."[2]

But, as with anything and everything in life, there's a right way and a wrong way to wield this feminine power. The Shulammite used it the way God designed: to entertain, ease tension, and reconcile with her husband. Unfortunately, some women use it to manipulate and exploit men.

> On Herod's birthday . . . the daughter of Herodias danced for them and pleased Herod so much that he promised with an oath to give her whatever she asked . . . Because of his oaths and his [dinner] guests, he ordered that her request be granted and [had] John beheaded in the prison. John's head was brought in on a platter and presented to the girl, who carried it to her mother. (Matthew 14:6, 9–11 BSB)

---

2. Douglas E. Rosenau, *A Celebration of Sex: A Guide to Enjoying God's Gift of Sexual Intimacy* (Nashville, TN: Thomas Nelson, 2001), 170.

In honor of Herod's birthday, Herodias's daughter Salome, gave Herod the birthday present of a lifetime—a smoking hot birthday performance in front of his envious buddies. Her racy exhibition stroked his male ego so profoundly, he promised to give her whatever her little heart desired—which to his shock and dismay, turned out to be the head of John the Baptist on a platter. Salome and her wicked mother, who coached her, knew full well that most men would sell their souls for a dance like the one she gave Herod. And Salome played him like a fiddle.

Mahanaim

Mahanaim (makh-an-eh') is an area in Gilead east of the Jordan River. It's the location where Laban chased Jacob down and confronted him about running off with his flocks, daughters, and grandchildren. It's also the same place Jacob had a face-off with his brother, Esau, years after cheating him out of his birthright. The common denominator in these conflicts is they both ended in peaceful reconciliation. Thus, Mahanaim gained the reputation as the place where two hostile camps came together—but left in peace.

The dance of Mahanaim is translated "the dance of two companies." It was known as a provocative dance done by one woman for one man. So what do we come up with if we merge an erotic dance with peaceful reconciliation? Simple, we come up with a sexy dance done as a prelude to make-up sex (*NIV Study Bible*, Genesis 32:2, fn., Genesis 32:13–21). How cool is that?

Abi's Story

Abi stands alone in their wedding chamber, clutching Solomon's note in her hand. She roams from room to room, basking in its familiarity.

Sweet-smelling bowls of exotic spices and flowers are scattered throughout the chamber. Even the pantry has been stocked with fine wine, raisin cakes, cheeses, olives, and choice fruits.

She fixes herself a small plate of savory goat cheese and a sliced pear, and pours a goblet of wine. Then sits on the marble bench beside the reflecting pool in the courtyard. This was one of her favorite spots. She always loved sitting out here in the cool of the evening watching the sky fade into darkness. Exhausted, she takes a few deep breaths. The wine is rich and pungent. So much has happened since this morning. It's hard to believe it was only a few hours ago that she woke up at the inn in the valley. It seems as if it was days ago.

Having eaten so little, the wine takes effect quickly. She slips into her nightclothes and crawls into bed. Lying there, she can't help but think about all the love they made in that bed. Tears stream down her face, soaking her hair and pillow. She cries out in prayer. "Father, I believed our marriage was dead and buried. I want to do the right thing. Truly I do. But, I don't know where to start. You promise to give beauty for ashes and bind the brokenhearted. Help me let go of the past. Give me strength. Help me forgive . . . Only you can breathe life back into our dead relationship. Amen."

Feeling God's loving presence, she drifts off to sleep.

Every morning Solomon delivers a heartfelt note or small trinket or gift, telling Abi that he is thinking of her—and only her. He suggests they ease into seeing each other with short meetings once or twice a week. She agrees.

Their first get-together is in the middle of the afternoon in the courtyard. They sit on benches facing one another. With her hands clutched in her lap, staring at the marble floor, she whimpers. "I was yours, and you were mine . . . We had something special . . . Something so few have." Looking up into his eyes, she asks. "What happened? You became distant . . . You were preoccupied . . . I thought it was a phase . . ." She stops to compose herself. "It seemed like you only came around when you wanted sex. I couldn't satisfy you anymore." Now sobbing and angry she adds, "Then . . . just like that . . . you abandoned me . . . You didn't even let me explain."

You're right, "I was preoccupied . . . I was consumed with building the palace," Solomon responds, "and the temple . . . I was angry when I left. I wasn't thinking straight. I'm so sorry . . . I wish I could go back and make it right. I wish I could take your pain away."

"I believe you. Or I wouldn't be here," she mutters. "But what really rips my heart out is . . . you stayed gone for so long. I'm not just hurt. I'm angry," she says through clenched teeth. "I'm so, so angry!"

Tears well up in his eyes, shamefully he admits, "It was never my intention to stay away . . . I got caught up in the smooth talk of the women . . . I was drunk on it."

"I just can't . . ." another extended pause "get the vision of you and all those women out of my mind." She wails, clinching a kerchief in her fists.

"I know. I know. I wish I could undo it," Solomon mourns, placing both hands on her shoulders and letting her cry herself out.

After she settles downs, he wipes her tear-soaked hair away from her eyes. "Take all the time you need. I'll be here." He rises and walks to the door. "Can I see you again in a few days?"

Staring into her lap, she nods.

Weeks later, after many more agonizing meetings, Solomon and Abi are walking through the colorful spring foliage of the palace gardens. Through a mischievous grin Solomon asks, "Remember the time we went horseback riding through the cedars and skinny-dipping under the waterfall?"

Abi laughs. "How could I forget? The horse ate my clothes while we were in the water! What a fun day that was. Those were happy times. I miss them."

Solomon stops and faces her. "Me too. We'll have times like that again. You'll see."

Their meetings get longer and closer together; each with fewer tears and more laughter. They find hope and joy in reminiscing about the good times. *Remember this? Remember that?*

"I hope we can do those things again," Abi sighs.

"We will," Solomon assures her. "You'll see." Then without warning he steals a quick, gentle kiss leaving her breathless.

A few weeks ago, Becca arrived at the palace to give her daughter emotional support. While the two of them are having breakfast, Abi tells her mother, "I'm beginning to sense that the time for Solomon and I to come back together is getting close."

"The only one who can know that is you," Becca replies. "Have you thought about how you want to go about it?"

Abi perks up. "I have. When he comes to one of our scheduled meetings, I'm going to surprise him with an amazing dinner and do the dance of Mahanaim for him. The next day we're going to disappear for a couple weeks on a romantic getaway."

"It sounds like you've put a lot of thought into it already," Becca replies. "Can I help?"

"Yes. New beginnings call for new bed coverings," Abi bubbles. "It'll be fun . . . just like before the wedding."

"It will be fun," her mother chimes. "When do you want to start?"

"Today," Abi chirps. "Let's get dressed and go to the trader's market and look for fabric."

Within a couple of hours, the ladies are at the market browsing and laughing. Abi finds a sheer, white Persian linen and green cording and tassels. The ladies sketch a billowy design and quickly begin sewing.

Several days later, they stand back and admire their work. "Oh, it's heavenly," Abi exclaims. At that moment a spark of desire flickers within her and she smiles.

"It is!" her mother agrees. "Do we make a great team, or what?"

The two ladies stand arm in arm and chant in unison, "We do," then break into laughter.

The next morning, during breakfast, Becca discloses her plans to return to the vineyard. "Sweetheart, you're doing so well . . . I really don't think you need me anymore. I've been away from the vineyard for a long time. I need to get back and make sure it's still standing."

"Oh, Ima, I understand," Abi replies. "Don't feel bad. I am better . . . I'm so much better. But I couldn't have done it without you. I appreciate you for coming. I'm going to miss you like crazy, though."

Not wanting to drag out her departure, Becca packs her belongings after breakfast and departs for home after lunch.

Feeling blue, Abi decides to cheer herself up. She digs through her cedar chest and finds the frame drum Aunt Lydia gave her for her ninth birthday. She taps out a simple rhythm. The cheerful jingle makes her smile. She fumbles through the dance of Mahanaim trying to recall the tune and steps. She persists until the movements begin to flow and become more graceful.

Abi continues planning her surprise getaway for Solomon. She finds a charming villa in the remote countryside and buys it, then makes arrangements to recreate their infamous horseback ride and swim under the waterfall. It will be a refreshing way to get out of the July heat.

After much probing at the market, she finally comes across a merchant with a mandrake and pays a ridiculous price for it. Upon returning to the palace, she drops in on her dear friend Abbott, the palace chef. The first time Abi met him, she felt a sweet bond between them. He took her under his wing like the father she never had.

UNLOCKING THE PAST

Mandrakes

Mandrakes are mentioned only twice in scripture; once in Genesis 30:14–16 and again in the Song. These scarce, quirky, uncultivated plants are found only near Jerusalem and Palestine. They look somewhat like lettuce, with deep purple flowers. They have a distinct fragrance and a potato-like fruit known as "love apples." However, what is quite comical is that their tan, carrot-like roots look very much like hairy, naked humans. And, according to folklore, when pulled from the ground, they scream. Our ancestors soaked the odd roots in wine and vinegar to leach out their highly sought-after aphrodisiac and fertility powers.

But please, don't get any crazy, harebrained ideas and try ordering these poisonous tubers online. Mandrakes are hallucinogens, and were frequently used to induce unconsciousness in surgery.

"Good day, Abbott," she says, kissing his chubby cheek. "I finally found this mandrake for the surprise romantic getaway I'm planning for Solomon. Would you mind storing it and keeping it alive for me?"

"Anything for my princess," he replies.

She hands him the potted mandrake and a long list of foods and wines. "Would you please have all these things delivered to the villa the day before we arrive?"

"It's as good as done," he assures her.

"Thank you, Abbott," she says, pressing her cheek against his. "Oh, and I almost forgot," she adds heading for the door, "pomegranates! I almost forgot pomegranates. Would you please add that to the list too?"

UNLOCKING THE PAST
Pomegranates

Hebrew legend has it that each pomegranate contained 613 seeds, one for each commandment in the Torah. The ruby-like seeds symbolize prosperity, marriage, and many children. This is why they were, and still are, given as wedding and housewarming gifts in the Middle East. Tradition has it that when couples got married or purchased a new home, pomegranates were broken open, exposing the hundreds of sparkling seeds inside—each seed representing a blessing.

Pomegranate images were used the same way we use four-leaf clovers for good luck, or hang horseshoes over our door posts to promote prosperity. However, this concept isn't based on superstition, it's actually biblical. Pomegranate ornamentation can be found throughout ancient architecture, including palace décor and minted coins. Jewish high priests were directed to embroider this logo of affluence and wealth onto the hems of their robes. Solomon was instructed to carve them into the capitals of the pillars in the temple (Exodus 28:33; 1 Kings 7:18-20).

"You got it, my dear. I'm so happy you and Solomon are working things out. If you need anything else, just let me know."

"What would I do without you?" Abi giggles.

Abi's surprise Mahanaim is less than two weeks away, but she still hasn't found anything suitable to wear for her sultry dance. One thing is for sure, it has to make her feel confident and sexy and it has to make Solomon weak in the knees. The next morning, she embarks on another shopping spree. This time she finds a green silk sash, lace-up sandals, and an exquisite gold necklace, bracelets, and earrings embedded with jade to pick up the green in her eyes.

Excited about her find, when she gets home, she heads straight to the bedroom and tries on her new ensemble. Looking in the mirror, she props her hands on her hips and boasts, "Girl, you still got it!"

By now the dance steps she has been practicing are coming effortlessly and without thought. Her practices are so fun and uplifting they have become the highlight of her day. But, as each day draws closer to their reunion, the butterflies in her stomach feel more like bats.

Abi makes one last trip to see Abbott. "Good morning, Abbott. How are you today?" she chirps, planting a peck on his cheek.

"Good morning Abi! Any day with you in it is a great day," he replies.

"My surprise Mahanaim is only three days away. In your expert opinion, what would you recommend for dinner?"

Without hesitation he replies, "I know just the thing. The king's new favorite is roasted duck with fig sauce and braised vegetables. Then for dessert, cinnamon-baked apricots topped with cherries, cream, and pecans. How does that sound?"

"I wasn't hungry till you said that," she says, licking her lips. "Also, here's another list of things I'll need: flowers, wine, fruit, spices . . . and four dozen lanterns."

"Four dozen lanterns?" Abbott repeats with a raised eyebrow.

"Yep." Giggling and blushing, "Four dozen lanterns."

"Will do," Abbott says with a chuckle, "Anything for my princess. What kind of flowers would you like?"

"Something white . . . Hydrangea if you can find them."

"You got it." He nods.

"Thank you. You're a sweetheart." After giving her usual smooch, she prances out the door.

The day has arrived. Abi wakes early and spends time in scripture and prayer. She is interrupted by a faint tapping on the door. Standing on the portico is a lanky teenage boy from the kitchen, surrounded by several carts loaded with gleaming silver lanterns, wine, and a basket of fresh fruit and spices.

"G-g-good morning, your highness. A-a-a-bbott sent these." The nervous lad stutters gesturing to the carts.

"Oh! Thank you!" Abi says, giving him her friendliest smile to put him at ease, "Would you please put them right here . . . in the vestibule?"

"As you wish, your h-h-highness."

Eager to start, she begins slicing pineapple, peaches, and apricots and drops them into a large elegant decanter along with a stick of cinnamon and vanilla bean. Then she fills the decanter with wine so the flavors can meld throughout the day.

Next, she spaces the lanterns a few feet apart into a trail, beginning at the front door and leading to the wedding chamber, then strategically arranges them around the perimeter of the room. She slides a couple of pieces of furniture out of the way, making room for her to dance. Lastly she places Solomon's favorite chair and a small table near the door.

After a light lunch, she relaxes in a luxurious, perfumed milk bath, and meditates on the passion they will once again share. As she applies her makeup and braids her tresses, Abi anticipates Solomon's sweet kisses and tender caresses.

There's a knock at her door. When she opens it, she is delighted to see Abbott's beaming face. "I wanted to deliver your dinner and flowers myself," he says brightly. "Can I help you set up?"

"Oh . . . Yes, yes. That would be so helpful," she says, opening the door wide.

With his professional flair, Abbott arranges the food tray, crisp white hydrangea, wine, and goblets on the table beside Solomon's chair. "Would you like me to light the lanterns for you?" he asks.

"Yes, yes, please," she replies.

The flames of the lanterns cast thousands of dancing shadows on the ceiling, walls and floor. "Everything is beautiful." Abbott says encouragingly. "May God bless you and Solomon tonight."

"Thank you, Abbott." Abi shrugs. "I'd be lying if I said I wasn't completely terrified."

"You're a beautiful and courageous woman. You're going to blow him away." And with those words, he turns and leaves her alone.

It's getting dark. He'll be here any minute, she thinks as a twinge of panic comes over her. She pours the wine into the goblets, takes a sip, smacks her lips, and says, "Perfect." Then she takes three generous gulps to calm her jitters.

She puts on her jade jewelry and sandals, removes her robe, and ties the sash of tiny white lilies around her naked hips. She opens an alabaster jar of nard, holds it to her nose and lingers in the luxurious fragrance, then strategically dabs it on from head to toe.

It's time, she says to herself, picking up her frame drum. Filling her lungs with air then exhaling the tension, she closes her eyes and begins tapping out the erotic rhythm of the dance of Mahanaim. As she listens and connects to the slow, suggestive tempo, her mind and body become one with the dance.

Several minutes later Solomon enters the dimly lit vestibule. Expecting their normal meeting, he pauses and cocks his head. Puzzled, he slowly follows the jingle of the hand drum and the trail of glowing lanterns down the corridor. Standing in the doorway, frozen in his tracks, he gawks in awe at Abi's nude form swaying in the flickering light, the white luminous marriage bed behind her.

Without missing a step she locks eyes with her beloved, and in a come-hither voice teases, *"Look with pleasure![3] How long has it been since you feasted your eyes on Solomon's girl doing the dance of Mahanaim?"* (Song 6:13b)

Mesmerized by her sultry movements, he slinks into his chair. Then he croons a ballad of wonder and gratitude:

> *"Oh, generous and willing[4] woman![5] How graceful are the steps of your sandaled feet! The curves of your hips and thighs are like jewels crafted by a cunning artisan. Your secret place[6] is a goblet that never lacks spiced wine. Your waist is like a sheaf of wheat[7] bound with lilies. Your breasts are like soft, twin fawns of a doe.* (Song 7:1-3)
>
> *"Your neck is elegant and resilient, like Lebanon's ivory tower watching over the enemy. Your face is serene. Your eyes are calm and lovely, like the deep green pools of Heshbon beside the gate of Bath-Rabbim!"*[8] (Song 7:4)

Abi rolls her slender body and flips her long tresses. He sings on:

---

3. Hebrew is *chazah*: to gaze or behold with delight
4. *nadiyb:* generous, noble, willing-hearted
5. *bath:* girl, sister, young woman, daughter
6. *shor:* vulva or secret place, a "euphemism for pudenda," Tremper Longman III, *Song of Songs,* The New International Commentary on the Old Testament (Grand Rapids, MI: Eerdmans, 2001), 194-95, Roland E. Murphy translates *shor* as "valley" and understands it as a "euphemism for the pudenda." See *The Song of Songs* (Minneapolis, MN: Fortress, 1990), 185.
7. *'arem*: an hourglass–shaped cluster of standing wheat, a sheaf
8. *Pools of Heshbon:* Reknown for their deep green fish ponds. The vast majority of Arabs have black or brown eyes, but if Solomon's compliment is literal, the Shulammite had green eyes.

"Your head crowns you like Carmel. Your swaying locks are like royal threads—I am captivated by your tresses. How beautiful and how pleasing you are, my darling. Your body is like a swaying palm tree; your breasts are like clusters of dates."(Song 7:5-7)

Solomon slowly rises from his chair and inches toward her, tenderly placing his hands on her bare waist. Brushing his cheek against hers, he whispers in her ear, *"I desire to climb*[9] *the palm tree and take hold of it fruit. I request*[10] *to embrace your breasts like clusters of dates on the vine. Your breath is fragrant as sweet apples and your kisses are like choice wine."*(Song 7:8-9a)

Abi whispers her consent, *"Come beloved, enter*[11] *my lips*[12] *and borders in peace.*[13] *Then we'll drift off to sleep. I am yours and you are mine."* (Song 7:9b-10)

After years of separation Abi and Solomon finally come together again, then lie peacefully entwined in each other arms, Abi tells Solomon about her surprise getaway, *"Come beloved. Let's escape to the countryside and spend the night in the hamlet. We'll get up early and go to the vineyard where passion may bloom. There I will give you my love. We will celebrate our love with sparkling pomegranates and love apples,*[14] *sending forth their aroma and passion. Inside those doors I have stored up old and new treasures for us to enjoy, my beloved."*(Song 7:11-13)

The next morning, they rise early and set out for the countryside to share two weeks of passion, solitude and intimacy, and to revive their new life together. Life is good again.

---

9. Hebrew is *alah:* to ascend or mount

10. *na':* to beseech or a modest request

11. *halak:* to come or enter, sometimes "to have intercourse with"

12. *saphah:* lips, shore, or natural boundary; the *labia majora* is known as the outer *lips* of the vulva

13. *meyshar:* sweetly, in agreement, and to make peace

14. *duwday*: love apples, mandrakes or "exciting sensual desire"

Making It Relevant

Betrayal

Anyone can have sex. Dogs can do that. But strong, well-rounded marriages are defined as husbands and wives who arduously interweave their emotions, personalities, dreams, strengths, flaws and bodies together with the other. I believe Solomon and the Shulammite were one of the few that experienced this rare type of relationship. Then Solomon, possibly bored or feeling he was entitled to more, was deceived into trading that precious oneness for the exhilaration of sex with a variety of women he barely knew. In time the thrill wore off. And what he took for granted and eventually wanted back, was the rare bond and intimacy he once knew with his best friend, soul mate and lover.

Wrongs cannot be reversed. Restoring broken trust after betrayal is agonizing in any situation—but it is especially difficult when it happens within the ultrasensitive realm of sexual intimacy. Trust cannot be promised forward. It must be scrupulously earned back. This is an incredibly painful process and requires a great deal of time, listening, understanding, and patience for the one left raw and bleeding from the betrayal. It also requires a tremendous amount of humility and accountability from the betrayer. Very few couples are able to overcome infidelity because both parties must remain willing and committed for the messy, uphill struggle.

Sex Etiquette and Mutual Consent

After editing and reading this manuscript over and over within a short period of time, I began to see connections evolving between the different love scenes. I noticed that on their wedding night, when the Shulammite was ready, she *invited* Solomon to come into his garden and he accepted her invitation. In the *Mahanaim* love scene, Solomon used the Hebrew word *na' halak*, which means "a modest, humble or unpretentious *request* to have intercourse with." She then granted him *permission* to enter her body. This decorum also holds true for the Proverbs 31 woman and the Proverbs 7 adulterous woman. Both *invited* their lovers into their bed for consensual sex. But then there's the polarizing scene where Solomon wakes the Shulammite up in the middle of the night and gropes her.

As I meditated over the various scenes, I noticed a "sex etiquette" thing taking shape. It seems that our Creator is trying to show us that there is a definite right way and wrong way for lovers to ask for sex. I believe this confirms that women's bodies were never meant to be "property" or "chattel," but sacred ground, to be entered with reverence and love. In my opinion, this is a matter that has been culturally biased for centuries. And something women, as well as men, should be taught a whole lot more of.

A Man's Desire

John Hagee, in his book *What Every Man Wants in a Woman*, cited earlier, polled the men of his congregation, "What are the top ten things you desire in a wife?" To no one's surprise, the number one answer was *sexual fulfillment*, and *recreational playmate* came in a close second.[15] Men want to be wanted. They enjoy sports and games, and they want sex to be a fun, playful adventure. They want you to let your hair down, throw caution to the wind, and rip their shirts off once in a while. Most wives understand sex is important to men, and accommodate their advances. But few women fully grasp how badly husbands want their wives to initiate uninhibited sex. In Dr. Joseph and Linda Dillow's and

15. John Hagee, *What Every Man Wants in a Woman*, 1–2 (see chap. 6, n. 6).

Dr. Peter and Lorraine Pintus's popular book *Intimacy Ignited,* they write: "Your husband wants you to desire him. Why? Because sexual intimacy affirms his masculinity. That's how God created him. One honest man said, 'For me respect is spelled S-E-X.'"[16]

To be fair, it's possible the Shulammite may have become lackadaisical over the years and slowly stopped initiating sex. If that's the case, it's possible her lack of interest might have made his adoring harem all the more enticing. Let me be clear: I am *not* excusing Solomon's poor choices. But let's face it, sooner or later, a half-starved person is going to give in to the thick, juicy steak.

Men Like to Look

Men are lookers. For whatever reason, God made them that way—on purpose. They're not unspiritual perverts. They're normal, testosterone-filled males. So, what happens when our husbands promise to only have eyes for us, but we don't give them anything to look at?

Shaunti Feldhahn's must-read book, *For Women Only*, give women a tell-it-like-it-is reality check of what men long for in a wife. Her research includes a poll of more than eight hundred men, half of which were churchgoers. Here is one of the questions she posed: "Imagine you are sitting alone in a train station and a woman with a great body walks in and stands in a nearby line. What is your reaction to the woman?"

Four percent said they would openly stare at her, and "drool forms on my lower lip."

Seventy-six percent said, "I'm drawn to look at her, and I sneak a peek or glance at her from the corner of my eye."

---

16. Joseph and Linda Dillow, Peter and Lorraine Pintus, *Intimacy Ignited: Fire Up Your Sex Life with the Song of Solomon* (Colorado Springs, CO: NavPress 2004) 114.

Eighteen percent said, "It is impossible not to be aware that she is there, but I try to stop myself from looking."

Two percent said, "Nothing happens; it doesn't affect me."[17]

Ouch! A whopping 98 percent said they couldn't help but be attracted to the woman. And here's the kicker: It didn't matter if they were happily married believers or not. The results were identical.

Let me attempt to put this into a perspective women can relate to. Wives also have itches that need scratching. We beg our husbands to listen, give flowers, help with the kids and household chores. But, are we willing to scratch *their* itch? To put it bluntly, they want to see you naked. If the Shulammite treated Solomon to a visual buffet, shouldn't we be willing to do the same for our husbands? Dress it up. Put a bow on it. Give your man a one-woman wet T-shirt contest. But for heaven's sake, let him look.

I've been warned about mentioning weight because it's damaging to a woman's self-esteem. So, I'll borrow a quote from a friend of mine who has struggled with weight her entire life. She put it this way: "Am I overweight because I have low self-esteem? Or do I have low self-esteem because I'm overweight?"

I'm not going to give you a pass and tell you it's okay to be out of shape and overweight. I'm not trying to get you to be svelte and model-thin either. I'm talking about health. In other words, is your *weight* causing high blood pressure, high cholesterol, diabetes, clogged arteries, joint or back pain, or a poor self-image? Are you able to walk up a couple flights of stairs without getting winded? Food disorders are not limited to bulimia and anorexia. If food controls you in any way, you have a food addiction—that includes obesity.

God calls us to aim for perfection (2 Corinthians 13:11 KJV). None of us will ever achieve perfection, but that shouldn't keep us

17. Shauti Feldhahn, *For Women Only: What you Need to Know about the Inner Lives of Men* (Atlanta: Multnomah, 2004) 113.

from aspiring to be. In other words, let's be careful we are not making excuses for things that *are* within our power to change or improve. On the flip side, should we allow ourselves grace? Absolutely. Some things we just have to make peace with and let it go. Wisdom lies somewhere in the beautiful balance.

In my first book, *Now That's Romantic!*, I encourage women, "Make one improvement. That improvement will spark another and another. Success breeds success. Before you know it, you'll love the woman looking at you in the mirror, and that ignites confidence. And confidence is sexy!"[18]

Creativity in the Bedroom

Is there anything worse than boredom? Doing the same thing day in and day out? Victor Hugo, the French poet and novelist, put it this way, "There is something more terrible than a hell of suffering—a hell of boredom."[19]

In Dillow and Pintus's book, *Intimacy Ignited,* they present us with an all too common, reoccurring complaint among married couples, "Everything about our lovemaking is familiar. The bedroom is familiar. Our bodies are familiar. He touches me, I touch him—always in the same way and the same place. Ten minutes later, it's over. This is supposed to be thrilling? How do we get out of this rut?"[20] This wife poses a very pertinent and common question. How do we escape monotony in the bedroom? Just how creative does God *allow* us to be?

Well so far, we've seen how the Shulammite danced naked, planned a romantic getaway, relived old favorites, and experimented with fun

---

18. Kim Moore, *Now That's Romantic!*, 38 (see chap. 2, n. 1).

19. Victor Hugo, *Les Miserables* (1822).

20. Dillow and Pintus, *Intimacy Ignited: Fire Up Your Sex Life with the Song of Solomon*, 239.

new things for them them to try. But what exactly were those old favorites and fun new things? We don't know. The Bible doesn't tell us.

In Esther 2, the harem girls were allowed to take one item with them to sleep with the king. Eager to make a wise choice, Esther consulted Hegai the eunuch to find out what the king enjoyed. What did he tell her? What did she take? We don't know. The Bible doesn't tell us. You've heard of Victoria's Secret? Well these are Shulammite's and Esther's secrets. Maybe they used a blindfold, chocolate finger paint, a large mirror, or an ancient sex toy. . . The point is, God left these a mystery on purpose. If He wanted us to know, He would have told us. He gives us the freedom to fill in the blanks with our imaginations. Don't be afraid to get creative.

To quote expert, Dr. Rosenau's book *A Celebration of Sex* again, he states, "Couples sometimes worry that certain props (like sexy lingerie, strategically placed mirrors, or vibrators) create artificial or sinfully seductive arousal and will detract from their natural lovemaking. God gave imaginations and romantic ability for us to create and enjoy various means of enticing and playing with our mates and props can be the means to enhance experiences and sensations."[21]

Fear

The word *create* means to produce something new and unique. But in order to do this, we have to get out of our comfort zone. And that's just plain scary. It's okay to feel fear, as long as we don't give in to it. Can you imagine how terrified virgin Esther must have been to sleep with a king who had been with so many women? It doesn't get any more intimidating than that. But here's the thing: I don't believe it was Esther's sexual prowess that won her the crown. I believe it was her

21. Douglas E. Rosenau, *A Celebration of Sex*: A Guide to Enjoying God's Gift of Sexual Intimacy (Nashville: Thomas Nelson, 2001), 71.

willingness to go the extra mile, to ask the tough questions, and the *courage* to follow through that made her stand out from the other girls. She may have even goofed up and looked silly, but that likely endeared her to the king all the more. Maybe they got a good laugh out of it and that's what made her memorable. True intimacy is being . . . vulnerable.

I say this cautiously because some will take this the wrong way, but when it comes to sex, many of us have been told that if something makes us feel uncomfortable, it must be wrong—that's not necessarily true. Growth is never easy. If you feel clumsy and awkward, you're probably doing something right. Change is hard. It doesn't matter if we're getting in shape, becoming financially independent, or learning a new skill. It's a long, arduous process, and there are no shortcuts. Development of any kind requires knowledge coupled with intentional, persistent action. And a red-hot love life is no different. If anything, it's harder. Seriously. Getting out of your comfort zone goes to an entirely new stratosphere when you're naked.

CHAPTER FOURTEEN

The Finale: The Next Generation

Our story comes full circle to the onset of the Shulammite's daughter's wedding. This chapter is a somewhat condensed version of the customs already outlined in chapters 1–3 of the Song. It starts with the betrothal and ends with the wedding banquet. I have given the Shulammite's daughter, the princess bride, the name *Sarai,* which means "my princess."

Parents: A large portion of this chapter is the Shulammite, who is now in the role of a mother, teaching her daughter lessons on the facts of life and marital commitment. It's an excellent tool and guideline to use when it comes time to prepare our teens for marriage.

[Princess Bride]

O that you were to me like a brother
who nursed at my mother's breasts!

If I found you outdoors, I would kiss you,
and no one would despise me.
I would lead you and bring you
to the house of my mother who taught me.
I would give you spiced wine to drink,
the nectar of my pomegranates.

[The Shulammite]

His left hand is under my head,
and his right arm embraces me.
O daughters of Jerusalem,
I adjure you:
Do not arouse or awaken love
until the time is right.
Who is this coming up from the wilderness,
leaning on her beloved?

I roused you under the apple tree;
there your mother conceived you,
there she travailed and brought you forth.

Set me as a seal over your heart,
as a seal upon your arm.
For love is as strong as death,
Its jealousy as unrelenting as Sheol.
Its sparks are fiery flames,
the fiercest blaze of all.
Mighty waters cannot quench love;
rivers cannot sweep it away.
If a man were to give all the riches of his house for love,
it would be utterly scorned.

[Brothers/Siblings]

We have a little sister,
and her breasts are not yet grown.
What shall we do for our sister
on the day she is spoken for?
If she is a wall,
we will build a tower of silver to protect her.
If she is a door,
we will enclose her with panels of cedar.

[The Princess Bride]

I am a wall
and my breasts are like towers.
So I have become in his eyes
like one who brings peace.

[The Shulammite]

Solomon had a vineyard in Baal-hamon.
He leased it to the tenants.
For its fruit, each was to bring
a thousand shekels of silver.
But my own vineyard is mine to give;
the thousand shekels are for you, O Solomon,
and two hundred are for those who tend its fruit.

You who dwell in the gardens,
my companions are listening for your voice.
Let me hear it!
Come away, my beloved,

and be like a gazelle
or a young stag
on the mountains of spices.
(Song 8:1-14 BSB)

History and Customs

The story evolves and begins again with the next generation. For that reason, there's not much new to learn in the way of history and customs.

At this point in the Song, the Shulammite's daughter has reached marrying age, so I'm guessing another seven or so years have passed since our last scene. Solomon has completed construction of the Lord's temple, his palace in Jerusalem, and several smaller palaces throughout the countryside. Through trade and strategic alliances with leaders in every corner of the known world, Solomon has transformed Israel into an economic and military powerhouse.

Before we continue our story, I'd like to remind you of a couple points mentioned at the beginning of the book. First, keep in mind that princesses were often promised to other kings or their sons at a very young age. However, the wedding would not take place until *after* she had sexually matured beyond puberty. It's probably not a stretch to assume that Solomon chose his future son-in-law very prudently. Only the best of the best would be good enough for his little girl. I would also like to believe he sought his daughter's wishes and opinions.

Second, it's important we remember that if a husband decided to marry additional wives without his wife or her father's consent, he was obligated to pay his first wife a minimum of fifty shekels of silver *for each additional wife he took*. I suppose it's possible, that since Solomon was so wealthy, the amount agreed upon in their *ketubah,* may have been substantially more.

Abi's Story

It's a cool crisp fall day at the palace. Abi's daughter, Sarai, has grown into a slender, dark-haired beauty like her mother. Sarai was promised to an outstanding, attractive and slightly older prince when she was only nine. But now, it's the day of her betrothal banquet and she has grown into a graceful, fifteen-year-old bride.

Abi, Sarai, and her bridesmaids are bustling about Sarai's room, getting ready for the banquet. Abi fastens the same heirloom mother-of-pearl necklace and earrings she wore at her betrothal around her daughter's neck.

Looking in the mirror and touching the piece ever so gently with her fingertips, Sarai exclaims, "Oh, Ima. It's such an honor to wear this. It's extraordinary."

"I felt the same way," Abi replies. "A long line of lovely, godly women have worn this necklace."

"I wore it too," Aunt Lydia boasts loudly.

"Well . . . how do I look? "Sarai asks, standing in her fuchsia dress. "Do you think the prince will be pleased?"

"Are you kidding? You're gorgeous!" answers one of her bridesmaids.

"You're going to take his breath away," her mother adds, her voice cracking.

Thrilled with her daddy's choice of groom, Sarai rattles on. "*O if only he was my brother, who nursed at my mother's breast, then if I ran into him on the street I could kiss him, and no one would ridicule me. I can't wait for him to carry me from my mother's house—from the one who teaches the delights of passion—and sweet intimacy.*" (Song 8:1-2)

"Oh, you sound just like me on the day of my betrothal, "Abi exclaims. "I remember it like it was yesterday." The girls draw close to listen to the queen's story. "The banquet was like a dream . . . everything was so beautiful and there were so many people . . . But when it was over, all of a sudden, Solomon and I found ourselves all alone . . . Solomon walked up to me and *put his left arm behind my head and his right arm around my waist and pulled me close.* (Song 8:3) The warmth of his body and his kiss left me breathless. I felt exactly the way you do. I, too, wanted to run away and live with him right then."

"You did? What did you do?" All the girls plead.

"My desire for him rose up in me so fast . . . I got scared. I was afraid if I didn't get away . . . I, I wouldn't be able to stop . . . that I'd do something I'd regret. So I squirmed out of his arms and I ran out of the hall like a bull."

Shocked at her tale, the girls gasp.

"Then guess what happened?" Abi prods.

"What, what?" the girls demand.

"I bolted out of the room so fast I knocked Solomon's best man, standing just outside the door, down into the dirt in front of three other groomsmen!"

The ladies roar with laughter.

"I was mortified! It had to be worst goodbye of all time!"

"I would have died!" said a bridesmaid.

"You can say that again. It haunted me for weeks," Abi jests. "You can bet that Solomon and his groomsmen laughed about it all the way back to the palace that night?"

"I sure hope my goodbye goes better than yours," Sarai jabs.

"So do I, my dear. So do I . . ." her mother agrees.

Then suddenly Abi's mood turns serious. Before we go, I want to finish my story with one last thought." Lovingly, she rests her gaze on each bridesmaid, then sings her legendary chorus, *"Daughters of Jerusalem, promise me you will not flirt or incite desire until the time comes to please your beloved, the one raised up for you in the wilderness."*[1] (Song 8:4-5)

---

1. Song 8:3–4 and 2:6–7 are identical, except the words "gazelles" and "does" are omitted.

UNLOCKING THE PAST
The Wilderness

In the Old Testament, the *wilderness* was frequently referred to as a time of training and testing in obscurity. It was a time when individuals were put through trials in preparation of their God-given purpose. Moses, David, John the Baptist, Joseph, Jesus, and many others all experienced a time of seclusion before coming forward and fulfilling their destinies. I believe the phrase *raised up for you in the wilderness* is referring to the young men or future husband God raises up for each of us.

However, keep in mind that the period of separation between the betrothal and wedding was also considered a form of wilderness training before entering the marriage covenant.

The girls enthusiastically reply in harmony. "We promise. We promise."

Abi smiles at Sarai, "You're so beautiful my dear. But now it's time for us to head down to the banquet hall. We wouldn't want to keep your groom and guests waiting."

Two months have passed since Sarai and her groom exchanged vows at their betrothal banquet before family and friends. The wind is howling about the palace on this wet, dreary December day. Sarai and Abi sit in one of the opulent guest rooms amid yards of lustrous silks, chatting and stitching bed coverings. Abi begins the first of her three-part lesson on the facts of life: foreplay, intercourse, and childbirth. She presents her lesson through a tender lullaby.

"Lying and aroused beneath my husband, there I conceived you, I labored, and gave you birth." (Song 8:5b) Expounding on her lesson she explains. "Foreplay is the strategy of kissing and touching. It's the

learned and skillful art of sensual pleasure between a husband and wife. It is deeply personal, vulnerable, and erotic, which is what makes it utterly holy. I don't want intimacy to come across as strictly physical or biological. So, the first thing I want to do is establish pleasant, easy-to-say analogies. For instance, instead of saying *aroused* or *hot,* we can use the word *spice,* and instead of *sex,* we'll refer to it as *eating* or *drinking.*" Instead of using the awkward word *vulva,* let's use the word *garden* or *secret place.* And instead of saying *wet,* we'll call it a *stream.* How does that sound? Does that make sense?"

Hanging on her mother's words and not realizing she has stopped stitching, Sarai nods intently.

"If you're anything like me, you're going to have a million questions," Abi assures her. "Don't be afraid to ask me anything. There's no such thing as a silly question. It'll get easier as we go. I promise."

Tongue-tied, Sarai stutters, "You're right: th-this *is* awkward." She pauses, then blurts out, "When my lover comes into my garden, will it hurt?" With a squeamish expression she adds, "Is it gross?"

Abi nods and answers calmly and matter-of-factly, "Those are great questions. As long as you don't rush . . . as long as you take your time and allow yourself to become fully aroused and your streams to flow . . . you should be fine. You may experience some tightness or slight discomfort, but it shouldn't hurt." Then, snickering, she continues, "I'm not going to lie. Sex can be messy. I suppose that's why the Law requires that couples bathe after sex. But messy is a good thing and we'll deal with messy more later. Now, that wasn't so bad, was it?"

"No . . . I guess not," Sarai replies sheepishly.

After a few more minutes of discussion, Abi decides to give her daughter time to digest what she has learned today and transitions to a lighter topic.

A couple of weeks later, Abi begins another lesson, "I think you're ready to heat things up a notch. Let's talk about what happens to our bodies during foreplay, shall we? But first, let's add a few more words to our vocabulary. Instead of using the word *penis,* we'll call it a *rod* or *tree.* When a man *releases his seed* or *ejaculates,* we'll call it his *fountain* or *flow.* Does that make sense?"

"Perfect sense," Sarai nods blushing.

"When a man kisses and caresses a woman—at least if he's taking his time and doing it right"—she rolls her eyes—"the stream in a woman's garden will begin to flow.

"Men get aroused much easier than women. All they have to do is look at a woman's naked body and they instantly become like a rod." They chuckle in unison. "When a man enters his wife's garden or secret place, his fountain will flow inside her."

"Oh, Ima," Sarai confesses nervously, "my stream is flowing just listening to you. Is that normal?"

"That's wonderful!" her mother encourages. "That's where sex begins for a woman—in her mind. It begins with thinking about intimacy with your husband. A great love-making session begins hours before you get in bed . . . It begins in your thoughts, while you are covering your bed and getting yourself ready."

"In fact, sometimes you won't feel like having sex. You'll be tired . . . or worried . . . or distracted about something. But, you'll be amazed how being intentional and thinking about making love can change your attitude. Pray about it. Do your hair or makeup. Put on something that makes you feel sexy. Dance! Dancing is a great turn on. It can radically change your mood and your state of mind."

They both giggle.

"Here's another little secret," Abi leans in and whispers. "If your husband knows you want him and desire him, you'll have him eating out of the palm of your hand." She teases giving her daughter and exaggerated wink.

"I definitely like the sound of that." Sarai chuckles.

After a dreadfully long winter, the sun finally comes out and warms the earth. Abi and Sarai decide to take advantage of the beautiful day and stroll through the gardens. Looking into the clear sky, Abi rejoices. "Isn't it wonderful to get outside after being cooped up all winter?"

"It is," Sarai nods in agreement. "The warm sunlight, the crisp air . . ." She inhales the fresh air and lets it out.

"It's been six months since your betrothal banquet, and I think you're ready to learn about orgasm. What do you think?"

"Are you kidding? This is what I've been waiting for!" Sarai squeals. "My curiosity is killing me."

Deep thought crosses Abi's face, "Orgasm is kind of difficult to describe. It starts out as small swells that roll in, each wave slightly bigger and stronger than the last. They slowly and rhythmically escalate and escalate . . . until it finally breaks forth in an intense flood of ecstasy."

Puzzled, Sarai asks, "How will I know if I'm having one?"

"Oh, honey, believe me. You'll know," Abi assures with an overstated nod and chuckle. "My advice is . . . when you feel the waves begin, relax into the moment and let go . . . surrender to them. Allow them to take over."

After several questions and answers, Abi wraps up her lesson. "Next week we will talk about the miracle of life . . . pregnancy and childbirth." She bubbles, "Oh, I just can't wait till you to make me a doting grandma!"

"Ima, I'm not even married yet and you're already going on and on about grandbabies."

"I admit it's premature," Abi giggles. "But I can't help myself. The thought of having little ones again is so exciting!"

A few weeks later, after breakfast, Abi and Sarai sit in the courtyard under a vivid blue sky among brilliant pink bougainvillea trellises. The sunshine is ideal for stitching beads and intricate handiwork onto Sarai's lavender silk wedding gown.

Today's lesson is about the commitment, hard work, and the often painful sacrifice it takes to succeed in a lifelong marriage. "Marriage is full of peaks and valleys, good times and bad." Abi begins, "But, no matter what, *wear your husband over your heart like a signet ring, or a seal on your arm. The love*[2] *between a man and a woman is as fierce as death. Its jealousy is as cruel as Hell . . . Its fury are the very flames of God's*[3] *wrath. Mighty waters cannot extinguish love, and floods cannot drown it out. If a husband were to give all the wealth of his house for love, it would be utterly despised."* (Song 8:6-7)

2. Hebrew is *'ahabah*: sexual love between a man and a woman

3. *shalhebeth Yahh:* flames of the LORD, *Jah-Jehovah*, The LORD most vehement

UNLOCKING THE PAST
Signet Rings and Seals

The Hebrew word for *seal* is *chowtham* and means "signet ring, seal, ownership or engraved in stone." A signet ring represented rank, position, or belonging and was worn on the hand or on a cord around the neck. In an article by Ashley Davis, titled "The History Behind . . . Signet Rings" Lori Ettlinger Gross explains, "Signet rings were used as seals, as a symbol or mark of the hand that sent or signed a document. Wax was melted onto the document and the top of the ring was impressed into the wax, leaving a clear and permanent mark. The top of the ring was usually set with a hard stone that had been deeply engraved with some kind of symbol or depiction."* The most common inscriptions were coats of arms, monograms, family seals, or initials (see Genesis 38:18).

In the Bible, seals were used to mark ownership on something precious or cherished. Wearing a seal on your arm demonstrated public pride and allegiance to a military cause or political view. As God's children, we are marked with the seal of the Holy Spirit (Ephesians 1:13).

*Ashley Davis, "The History Behind . . . Signet Rings," *National Jeweler*, September 7, 2016, https://www.nationaljeweler.com/fashion/antique-estate-jewelry/4637-the-history-behind-signet-rings-2.

That evening, Abi, Sarai, and her older brothers are sitting beneath the massive, gold chandelier in the family dining room, finishing up supper. As they dialogue about the impending wedding, the conversation takes a turn as Sarai's older brothers begin to tease her relentlessly. *"Remember when she was just a flat-chested little girl and we used to wonder, 'What shall we demand for our sister when she is old enough to be spoken for? If she is a virgin,*[4] *we will demand a bride price equal to towers*

4. Hebrew is *chowmah:* a wall, euphemism, a chaste or unapproachable woman

of silver. But, if she is flirtatious and coy,[5] *we will set boundaries around her and shelter her.'"*(Song 8:8-9)

Not amused at her brothers' jabs, Sarai defends herself. *"I've done perfectly well at keeping myself chaste. I've grown up and I'm ready to marry. Since then I have become*[6] *a mature woman*[7] *in the eyes of my beloved, eager to bring him happiness and contentment."* (Song 8:10)

Late fall has set in. The ladies wake up to a sparkling cloak of frost covering the palace and grounds. The anniversary of the betrothal is just two days away. In final preparation of the carry, Sarai and her mother have a full day of work packing her trousseau, wedding dress, and bed coverings. The guest room is covered from one end to the other with beautiful belongings the bride has accumulated for their new life together. They admire and comment on each item before they carefully pack it away.

Abi has one last lesson for Sarai, one she'd rather not discuss. Sarai notices that her mother has recently become quiet and not her cheerful self. "Ima, is something wrong? You're so quiet . . ."

Abi stops folding the tunic in her hand, sits on the bed, and pats the spot next to her, bidding her daughter to join her. She takes hold of her hands and exhales noisily. "Sarai," she begins, "being a queen—the wife of a king—is not as glamorous or as easy as most people think. It has its share of unique challenges." She takes another painful pause. "You need to understand it is very possible your prince may

5. Hebrew is *deleth:* a door, euphemism, flirtatious and coy, an easily accessible woman

6. *hayah*: to appear in someone's eyes, to be a woman, to lie with

7. *shad migdal:* mature breasts and ready for marriage

take other wives . . . and someday you may have to share his affections with others."

"I know," Sarai says glumly. "I try not to think about that . . . I keep hoping it won't be like that for us."

"I hope so too," her mother says with an optimistic smile. "Sharing your father is the hardest thing I've ever had to do. It's no secret that *Solomon is*[8] *the husband*[9] *of hundreds*[10] *of wives and concubines and he lies with them. Each was purchased*[11] *with a thousand shekels of silver.*[12] *Nevertheless, my body is mine. A thousand shekels of silver were for Solomon, but two hundred shekels*[13] *are reserved for me to compensate for my loss.*"(Song 8:11-12)

The Grand Finale

Sarai's wedding day has finally arrived. Her prince groom came shortly past midnight and swept her from the palace. The carry to her father-in-law's estate was almost a mile long, with thousands of torches illuminating the night sky.

Sarai and her mother, her great-aunt Lydia, and her bridesmaids have been celebrating and assisting the bride all day. It's been a delightful, lighthearted day filled with memories and laughter. It's mid-afternoon and the girls are helping Sarai into her bridal gown, crown and veil. The women marvel at her beauty and shower her with compliments.

---

8. Hebrew is *hayah*: to marry or possess
9. *hamon*: lord, husband, and master
10. *baal:* (see Judges 2:17 NIV Study Bible footnote). Also meant *lord* and *husband*, and a metaphor for *adultery*.
11. *nathan:* to give, lay, entrust
12. *thousand shekels of silver:* the bride-price Solomon paid for each bride. BibleHub.com footnote, 25.1 pounds or 11.4 kilograms of silver
13. *two hundred shekels:* the penalty owed for wives taken without consent

"You are perfect from head to toe," a bridesmaid coos.

Slowly shaking her head in wonder, Abi sniffs. "I don't think it's possible to be any more beautiful."

"She's the most breathtaking bride I've ever seen!" Aunt Lydia bellows. "She's even more beautiful than you on your wedding day."

Abi cups Sarai's chin in her hands and whispers, "They'll be coming to get you for the wedding procession any minute." Large tears slide down her cheeks. "It's time for me to let you go."

Cherishing the moment, Abi gives her daughter a long embrace. Stepping back she takes Sarai's hand with her right hand and another bridesmaid's hand with her left. The bridesmaids follow suit taking each other's hands until they form a circle. Abi lovingly rests her gaze on each girl, ending with her daughter. Then she speaks a joyful, yet resolute decree over them, *"Brides and bridesmaids of all generations waiting to marry, listen, discern, and obey the things I've taught you. Hear my declaration of happiness! Flee with your beloved like a young doe and stag, to the holy mountains of passion."* (Song 8:13-14)

THE END

Making It Relevant

The Shulammite's Blessing

The Shulammite's powerful closing words over the bridesmaids give brides of all generations not only the authority to embrace our roles as wives and lovers, but the permission to enjoy passionate and playful sex.

For centuries women have been made to feel ashamed of their sexuality. It's my hope and dream that we, the Daughters of Jerusalem, will no longer allow the false religious narratives of the past to impair our marriages and families. Going forward we will boldly and confidently step into our femininity as strong, godly women—strong physically, mentally, emotionally, spiritually, financially, and *sexually.* It's time for women to grasp the concept that a healthy female identity is every bit as essential as smart nutrition, physical exercise, mental and emotional health, and financial independence.

What a Disappointing Ending!—Or is It?

You're probably thinking, *If Solomon took all those wives and concubines, then the Shulammite's story ended terribly.* For quite some time I felt the same way, but then I realized that even though the Song was over, Solomon and the Shulammite lived many more years, so their story was not over. I believe that the following words, penned by Solomon, give us a clue to their ultimate ending. I'm wholeheartedly convinced that the woman Solomon speaks of as the "wife of his youth" in the passage below, (see vv. 5:18-19) is no other than the lovely Shulammite. Surely, the woman he speaks of is the same one who captured his heart in the Song, and the same one to have an entire opera written in her honor.

[Solomon]

My son, pay attention to my wisdom;
incline your ear to my insight,
that you may maintain discretion
and your lips may preserve knowledge.
Though the lips of the forbidden woman drip honey
and her speech is smoother than oil,
in the end she is bitter as wormwood,
sharp as a double-edged sword.

Her feet go down to death;
her steps lead straight to Sheol.
She does not consider the path of life;
she does not know that her ways are unstable.

So now, my sons, listen to me,
and do not turn aside from the words of my mouth.
Keep your path far from her;
do not go near the door of her house,
lest you concede your vigor to others,
and your years to one who is cruel;
lest strangers feast on your wealth,
and your labors enrich the house of a foreigner.
At the end of your life you will groan
when your flesh and your body are spent,
and you will say, "How I hated discipline,
and my heart despised reproof!
I did not listen to the voice of my teachers
or incline my ear to my mentors.
I am on the brink of utter ruin
in the midst of the whole assembly."

Drink water from your own cistern,
and running water from your own well.
Why should your springs flow in the streets,
your streams of water in the public squares?
Let them be yours alone,
never to be shared with strangers.
May your fountain be blessed,
and may you rejoice in the wife of your youth:
A loving doe, a graceful fawn—
may her breasts satisfy you always;

may you be captivated by her love forever.
Why be captivated, my son, by an adulteress,
or embrace the bosom of a stranger?
For a man's ways are before the eyes of the LORD,
and the LORD examines all his paths.
The iniquities of a wicked man entrap him;
the cords of his sin entangle him.
He dies for lack of discipline,
led astray by his own great folly.
(Proverbs 5:1-23 BSB)

Chasing After the Wind

If there was ever anyone who had an ostentatious and endless list of accomplishments to brag about, it was Solomon. He chased the winds of never-enough—including and especially women (Ecclesiastes 2:10–11). He denied himself no pleasure. Yet at the end of his days, when all was said and done, he realized everything he had accomplished was hollow, meaningless and purposeless—a "chasing after the wind." You can hear the sadness and remorse in his words, as he implores his sons to learn from his experiences and to choose a better way. To hold on to the one and only woman who can truly make them happy: their first true love, best friend and soul mate.

At first I thought, *If Solomon was the wisest man to ever live, then he obviously never made poor choices. Right?* No, that's not necessarily so. Just because God anointed him king and granted him wisdom did not mean he lived a perfect life. Solomon was flawed, deeply flawed. Let's face it, he did some highly questionable things during his lifetime. He put his own brother to death, used slave labor, blatantly disobeyed God by making trade deals with Egypt and slept with a thousand women.

Like Solomon, all our heroes of the Bible were flawed. David was a great warrior and king, but he committed adultery with Bathsheba then murdered her husband to cover it up. He was also a lousy father. Yet God said he was a man after his own heart.

Moses was a murderer and had a short fuse, yet he rescued the Israelites from Egypt via the Red Sea and God described him as the humblest man on the face of the earth.

Peter had a potty mouth and liked to fight. He even adamantly denied knowing Jesus. Not once, not twice, but three times. Yet, only fifty days after his contrite denial, Peter delivered the first gospel sermon on the Day of Pentecost and Jesus established him as the "Rock" that His church would be built upon (Matthew 16:18).

Every single one of God's chosen had major flaws and failures with highly questionable pasts. Had any of them lived today, the media would have eaten them alive. Every last one of them would have been discredited and branded inadequate and corrupt. Yet God used them as the pillars of our faith.

Godly men and women fail miserably. But they come to their senses, repent and *finish* well. The book of Ecclesiastes shows us that when Solomon approached his later years, his wisdom returned to him and according to the afore-mentioned passage, I believe he returned to the wife of his youth. And, before it was all said and done, he and the Shulammite lived happily ever after.

CHAPTER FIFTEEN

"Who Told You That You Were Naked?"

In the Garden of Eden, Adam and Eve were frolicking around in the buff, basking in paradise when the serpent quietly slithered into their lives and sweet-talked them into sampling the forbidden fruit. Suddenly they felt guilty and ashamed, and for the first time realized they were naked, so they covered their private parts with big, scratchy fig leaves.

When God went for His usual evening stroll through the garden, Adam and Eve heard Him approaching, and because they felt guilty for disobeying, they hid. God called out, "Where are you?"

Adam replied, "I was afraid because I was naked. And I hid."

God asked, "Who told you you were naked?" (Genesis 3 MSG)

In essence what God was asking was, "You've been naked all this time. Now, all of a sudden you think it's wrong. Why? Who told you that you were naked? *Who told you naked is wrong?*"

My questions to you are similar: Who told you that sex on Sunday is wrong? Who told you anything other than the missionary position is wrong? Who told you lingerie and stilettos are wrong? Who told you ____________ was wrong?" (Fill in the blank with whatever you may have been taught or led to believe.) Now, here's the test: Do you have chapter and verse to support your beliefs? Have you read and studied the text for yourself? Was the scripture used in context? Does it line up with other scriptures? Does it line up with the Song?

One thing I've learned about God is He *never* minces words on crucial issues. In fact, when something is important, He repeats Himself many times in various ways to drive home His point. And, when it comes to sexual boundaries, He's repetitive and crystal clear. If you are not familiar with Biblical sexual boundaries, I have compiled a list of scriptures in appendix 2 for your convenience.

Test Everything

Many people claim the Bible contradicts itself, and for decades I would have agreed. But not anymore. Looking back now, I can see that many of those "contradictions" or "inconsistencies" were the result of being taught an erred or distorted doctrine, during the early, foundational years of my faith. In fact, as a brand-new Christian, the church I was converted in, taught that their interpretation was the only correct doctrine and I should not listen to any teachings except theirs. And to compound matters, they used scripture to convince me that being unwavering (close-minded) was a virtue! As a result, I was unteachable for decades.

> Don't believe everything you hear. Carefully weigh and examine what people tell you," (1 John 4:11 MSG).

Wise Christians listen and learn from older, wiser Christians. But, just because someone is older and wiser doesn't mean that person is right about everything, all the time. People are fallible. Even the most good-hearted, God-fearing people get things misconstrued. They don't do it on purpose. They simply *assume* that what they were taught was correct and neglect to test it for themselves. Then they carelessly pass wrong information on to others.

Unlike those living in the Dark Ages, we are without excuse. Today we have every translation of the Bible at our disposal online—for free. We even have Hebrew and Greek dictionaries to do our own digging and research. It is our personal responsibility to test and filter everything we learn through the Word of God in *independent* study. This is God's way of setting checks and balances. This doesn't mean we should be confrontational, divisive, or cynics. But, it doesn't mean we should sit back and be spoon fed either. It's all about balance and maturity.

God refers to His Word as a mystery—an intricate and infinite puzzle. But what happens if, at the beginning of our faith, we take someone's teaching as absolute truth and put pieces of our puzzle in the wrong places? Sooner or later, we won't be able to finish our puzzle—at least, not until we realize we made a mistake somewhere along the line. At that point we must backtrack and find the misplaced pieces. Only then can the pieces be put in their correct places so the puzzle, the complete and perfect picture, can be seen.

If your interpretation of the Bible contradicts itself, or has holes in it, it's a good bet you've put some of your puzzle pieces in the wrong places. Be willing to listen to new viewpoints in light of ***all*** scripture. And keep adjusting your puzzle pieces until everything fits in harmony with everything else.

> Do not treat prophecies with contempt but test them all. (1 Thessalonians 5:20–21)

> Now the Berean Jews were of more noble character than those in Thessalonica, for they received the message with great eagerness and examined the Scriptures every day to see if what Paul said was true. (Acts 17:11)

Paul was an apostle, and God endorsed his message with miracles. Yet Paul didn't get bent out of shape when the Bereans double-checked his message against the Old Testament to see if it was true. To the contrary, he applauded them for having the integrity to do so. Shouldn't we be doing the same? Do it with this book. Check it out for yourself; examine the scriptures and my resources.

We Need a Cure, Not a Band-Aid

What does it mean when a survey conducted by the Barna Group concluded that Christians rank no better than non-Christians in divorce?[1]

What does it mean in an article in *Today's Christian Woman* that 46 percent of churchgoers believe we need more practical, biblical sex education from the pulpit?[2]

What does it mean when liberal Planned Parenthood conducted a survey of women seeking their services, and only a scant 5 percent reported having received any form of parental sex education?[3]

What does it mean when men in the church, including those in leadership, continue to struggle with pornography?[4]

---

1. Barna, "Born Again Christians Just as Likely to Divorce as Are Non-Christians," Barna Research, accessed June 26, 2020, https://www.barna.com/research/born-again-christians-just-as-likely-to-divorce-as-are-non-christians/.
2. Cindy Crosby, "The Best Sex (Survey) Ever!" *Today's Christian Woman*, September 2008, https://www.todayschristianwoman.com/articles/2008/september/best-sex-survey-ever.html.
3. Tommy Nelson, *The Book of Romance: What Solomon Says About Love, Sex, and Intimacy* (Nashville, TN: Thomas Nelson, 1998), 88.
4. "You are here: Home U.S. Shocker: Study Shows Most Christian Men Are Into Porn," *Charisma News*, October 7, 2014, https://www.charismanews.com/us/45671-shocker-study-shows-most-christian-men-are-into-porn.

What does it mean, according to the National Survey of Christian Female Sexuality, that nearly one-third of married women are sexless?[5] ("Sexless" is defined as having sex fewer than ten times a year.) If this is true, what percentages of marriages are active—but miserable? When miserable marriages are undealt with, they often fester into adultery, pornography, and divorced and shattered families. The scripture rings true, "They dress the wound of my people as though it were not serious" (Jeremiah 6:14; 8:11).

In Dillow and Pintus's previously mentioned book *Intimacy Ignited,* they cite this shocking testimony: "Eleven years ago, my wife stood before me and said, 'I will never have sex with you again.' Eleven years of living in the same house yet miles apart . . . Sometimes we mistakenly believe that people who follow Christ are protected from such tragedy, but this man and his wife are both respected leaders in their church. He is a pastor and preaches every Sunday. She sings on the worship team. They haven't had sex in seven years . . . 'People see us in church and think we are a happy, godly family. If only they knew . . .'"[6]

Christians need a cure, not a Band-Aid. Complacency and denial are no longer acceptable. The world flaunts their views of sex at every opportunity. It's discussed anywhere and everywhere—everywhere except where it should be—at home and at church. If Christians don't teach it, where will we get our information? Social media? *Cosmo*? The public school system? The problem with most Christians is, we don't know what we don't know. We are unconsciously incompetent. We own the equipment, but we have no idea how to use it.

---

5. Archibald D. Hart, Catherine Hart Weber, Debra Taylor, *Secrets of Eve: Understanding the Mystery of Female Sexuality,* (Nashville, TN: Word Publishing, 2004) 164, 65.

6. Joseph and Linda Dillow, Peter and Lorraine Pintus, *Intimacy Ignited: Fire Up Your Sex Life with the Song of Solomon* (Colorado Springs, CO: NavPress 2004) 102.

From the very beginning God established marriage as one man and one woman, and to be fruitful and multiply. Sex is the unique bond and secret place that sets marriage above all other relationships. Marriage is the covenant that two people share and build a life and the nuclear family upon. And, that's precisely why the enemy went for the jugular when he targeted the Song. He knew if he could strip the Song of its meaning, it would throw us into confusion. He knew if he could strip the Song of its authority, we would be defenseless. He knew if he could create mayhem in the secret place nobody wants to talk about, he could undermine marriages, families, and ultimately, the world. I don't know about you, but that makes me fighting mad. It's time we take back what's rightfully ours. I'm convinced it's time for a biblical sexual revolution.

It's my dream that this new understanding of the Song will bring the church's silence to a grinding halt. I hope that being able to see "marital sex" in black and white in the Bible, will give couples the courage, tools and authority they need to enjoy sex without shame or guilt. And to help others do the same. I dream of the day Christian marriages become so playful and affectionate, the world will want what we have.

Too often we learn something like this, but do nothing with it. Do you lead a marriage group? Do you mentor teenage girls? Do you teach a women's group? Do you counsel married and engaged couples? Do you have daughters? Nieces? Granddaughters? Is there anyone, including men, who can't benefit from understanding the Song?

It's called the Song of all Songs for a reason. Let's start teaching the entire Word of God—including and especially the Song. Change begins one person at a time, one marriage at a time, one bedroom at a time. Amen.

APPENDIX 1
THE DARK AGES: TIME LINE

AD 380 Emperor Flavius Theodosius declared Rome a "Christian" empire and instituted the Catholic Church as its exclusive religion.

382 The New Testament was translated from the original Greek into Latin, known as the Latin Vulgate. Latin, however was not a language used in society; it was learned and used solely by the priests.

476 The Western Roman Empire collapsed and the Church filled the void and stepped into power, making the empire a theocracy.

500 At that time, individual books of scriptures were available in more than five hundred languages. However, the Church established a law that the Latin Vulgate was the official scripture of the Church, thereby making it illegal for lay persons to possess scripture. If you did not surrender non-Latin scripture, you could be executed.

600 The only scripture available was the Latin Vulgate.

1229 The Council of Toulouse prohibited the common man from reading and interpreting scripture. The article reads, "We prohibit also that the laity should be permitted to have the books of the Old and New Testament; unless anyone from motive of devotion should wish to have the Psalter or the Breviary for divine offices or the hours of the blessed Virgin; but we most strictly forbid their having any translation of these books."

1380 John Wycliffe, Oxford Professor: With the help of his followers, the "Lollards," they translated and hand copied the English Bible from the Latin Vulgate.

1415 John Hus, a Wycliffe follower: Opposed the Church and was burned at the stake using Wycliffe's transcripts as kindling.

1428 Pope Martin V: Was so furious with Wycliffe that forty-four years after his death, he had his bones exhumed, burned, crushed, and thrown into the Swift River.

1450 Johannes Gutenberg: Invented the Gutenberg movable-type printing press.

1517 Martin Luther: Nailed his *Ninety-five Theses of Contention* to the church door at Wittenberg. He also translated and published the first German Bible. William Tyndale, Myles Coverdale, and John Rogers also helped translate the Old and New Testaments into English, German, and other languages.

1535 On October 4th, the first complete English Bible, the Coverdale Bible, was printed and put in circulation.

THE DARK AGES: PHILOSOPHIES TAUGHT

Plato (427–347 BC), Greek philosopher, student of Socrates. Taught that the means to higher spirituality was to abolish sensual desire. Catholic priests, bishops, and popes embraced his ideologies and continued to expound on them. The word *platonic* is derived from his name.

Ambrose (339–397), bishop of Milan, Doctor of the Church. Taught it was better for mankind to cease to exist than to succumb to the depravity of sexual intercourse.

Jerome (347–420), a priest and Doctor of the Church. Translated the New Testament from the Greek into Latin. He believed sexual desire was so vile that when he felt it come upon him, he would throw himself onto thorny bushes.

Origen (184–254), a Christian theologian and Doctor of the Church. Taught catechisms to young women. It's believed he was so fixated with the evils of sex that he castrated himself and rewrote the Song of Solomon as an allegory.

Augustine of Hippo (354–430), bishop and Doctor of the Church. Lived an exceptionally promiscuous young-adult life. After his conversion, he vehemently denounced sex and vowed to live a life of celibacy. He expounded on the doctrine of "original sin" and taught that Adam and Eve's great transgression in the Garden of Eden was sexual intercourse.

APPENDIX 2
SCRIPTURES ON SEXUAL RELATIONS

Do not dishonor your father by having sexual relations with your mother. She is your mother; do not have relations with her.

Do not have sexual relations with your father's wife; that would dishonor your father.

Do not have sexual relations with your sister, either your father's daughter or your mother's daughter, whether she was born in the same home or elsewhere.

Do not have sexual relations with your son's daughter or your daughter's daughter; that would dishonor you.

Do not have sexual relations with the daughter of your father's wife, born to your father; she is your sister.

Do not have sexual relations with your father's sister; she is your father's close relative.

Do not have sexual relations with your mother's sister, because she is your mother's close relative.

Do not dishonor your father's brother by approaching his wife to have sexual relations; she is your aunt.

Do not have sexual relations with your daughter-in-law. She is your son's wife; do not have relations with her.

Do not have sexual relations with your brother's wife; that would dishonor your brother.

Do not have sexual relations with both a woman and her daughter. Do not have sexual relations with either her son's daughter or her daughter's daughter; they are her close relatives. That is wickedness.

Do not take your wife's sister as a rival wife and have sexual relations with her while your wife is living. (Leviticus 18:7–18)

Do not have sexual relations with a man as one does with a woman; that is detestable. (Leviticus 18:22)

Do not degrade your daughter by making her a prostitute . . . (Leviticus 19:29)

If a man commits adultery with another man's wife—with the wife of his neighbor [it is a sin]. (Leviticus 20:10)

If a man has sexual relations with his father's wife, he has dishonored his father . . .

If a man has sexual relations with his daughter-in-law . . . [w]hat they have done is a perversion . . .

If a man has sexual relations with a man as one does with a woman, both of them have done what is detestable . . .

If a man marries both a woman and her mother, it is wicked . . .

If a man has sexual relations with an animal, [it is a sin] . . .

If a woman approaches an animal to have sexual relations with it, [it is a sin] . . .

If a man marries his sister, the daughter of either his father or his mother, and they have sexual relations, it is a disgrace . . .

If a man has sexual relations with a woman during her monthly period, he has exposed the source of her flow, and she has also uncovered it . . .

Do not have sexual relations with the sister of either your mother or your father, for that would dishonor a close relative . . .

If a man has sexual relations with his aunt, he has dishonored his uncle . . .

If a man marries his brother's wife, it is an act of impurity; he has dishonored his brother. (Leviticus 20:11–21)

"But I tell you that anyone who looks at a woman lustfully has already committed adultery with her in his heart." (Matthew 5:28)

"For it is from within, out of a person's heart, that evil thoughts come—sexual immorality, theft, murder, adultery, greed, malice, deceit, lewdness, envy, slander, arrogance and folly." (Mark 7:21–22)

In the same way the men also abandoned natural relations with women and were inflamed with lust for one another. Men committed shameful acts with other men, and received in themselves the due penalty for their error. (Romans 1:27)

It is actually reported that there is sexual immorality among you, and of a kind that even pagans do not tolerate: A man is sleeping with his father's wife. (1 Corinthians 5:1)

Or do you not know that wrongdoers will not inherit the kingdom of God? Do not be deceived: Neither the sexually immoral nor idolaters nor adulterers nor men who have sex with men. (1 Corinthians 6:9)

It is God's will that you should be sanctified: that you should avoid sexual immorality. (1 Thessalonians. 4:3)